Legends
Oddities
& Mysteries

... including
UFO experiences
in New Brunswick

by Dorothy Dearborn

illustrated by Carol Taylor

An Original New Brunswick Paperback from
Neptune Publishing Company Ltd. Saint John

A paperback original from Neptune Publishing Company Ltd.

10 9 8 7 6 5 4

Legends, Oddities & Mysteries
... including UFO experiences
in New Brunswick

Canadian Cataloguing in Publication Data
ISBN 1 – 896270 – 06 – 9

Dearborn, Dorothy
Legends and oddities and Mysteries from New Brunswick
Curiosities and wonders – New Brunswick
2. Legends -- New Brunswick. I. Title.
FC2461.8.D42 1996 001.9'4' 097151 C96–950037–8
F1042.6.D42 1996

Illustrations by Carol Taylor
Cover design by Dorothy Dearborn
Typesetting & book design by Dearborn Group, Hampton, NB

Neptune Publishing Company Ltd.
116 Prince William Street, Box 6941
Saint John, NB E2L 4S4

Acknowledgements

The importance of the support of those who have contributed to or assisted in my research for this book is impossible to stress. A simple 'thank you' seems inadequate. Without you this book could not have happened. I thank you for more than the opportunity to delve into your memories and memorabilia. I thank you for the experience and for the pleasure of meeting many of you for the first time. Perhaps I should be amazed at the support and help so many have provided me, but I stopped being amazed a long time ago because this is New Brunswick after all. It's the way you are and the way I hope I am when you or others look to me for similar support.

There are those who are there for me every time I set out on a project. They include my family, of course; Liza Aitkin of the *Fredericton Gleaner* archives, the staff of the Saint John Regional Library and Joanne Cadogan of the *Miramichi Leader* who has a genius for pointing me in the direction of a good Miramichi story or two.

The names found on the following pages are the names of real, not fictional persons. People who shared their stories and donated their valuable time to allow me to interview and quote them. A very special thank you to all.

In addition, a number of people, whose names do

not appear as sources, have been extremely supportive in the research of a number of stories herein. They include C. Konrad Buczynski, Bev. Hazlett, Fenton Doak, David Robertson, Barry Toole and Mary Flagg.

The Telegraph Journal and The Evening Times Globe newspapers as well as the Daily Gleaner were the source of some of the stories in this book . In addition I acknowledge taking the liberty of quoting from, or suggesting the reading of, books by Doris Calder and the late Stuart Trueman, both of whom have made valuable contributions to the documentation of New Brunswick history.

Other special acknowledgments are included in the introduction to the section on UFOs in New Brunswick.

Thank you all,

Dorothy Dearborn,
Hampton, NB
March 31, 1996

Contents

Other books by Dorothy Dearborn

<u>Young Adult</u>
The Secret of Pettingill Farms
Avalon Books, New York 1972
The Mystery of Wood Island
Avalon Books, New York 1973

<u>Biographies</u>
Give Me Fifteen Minutes Roy Alward of Havelock
Unipress Limited, Fredericton 1978
Dyslexia Dr. Arthur Chesley, Saint John
Dearborn Group, 1992

Anthologies
Willie (A Short Story)
Stubborn Strength A New Brunswick Anthology
by Michael O. Nowlan
Academic Press Canada, 1983

<u>Collections</u>
Partners in Progress, New Brunswick
Atlantic Canada–At the Dawn of a New Nation
Windsor Publications Ltd. Burlington, Ontario 1990

<u>Non-Fiction</u>
Unsolved New Brunswick Murders
Neptune Publishing Company Ltd. 1993
New Brunswick Ghosts, Demons
... and things that go bump in the night
Neptune Publishing Company Ltd. 1994
Madness and Murder
Neptune Publishing Company Ltd. 1995

Preface

When I first began researching the material for this book I discovered that it was impossible to really focus on one sector. Every time I tried someone came up with a fascinating story that screamed to be told, or with a new twist to an old story that begged to be included. The result is what you see here, *Legends, Oddities & Mysteries … including UFO experiences in New Brunswick*.

If an occasional story appears to be a many told tale I suggest a closer read as old tales may include new information …among these are the stories of the Christ Church Cathedral ghost in Fredericton and Moncton's famous Magnetic Hill.

If the inclusion of the Bricklin story does not, at first glance, appear to fit any of the listed categories, read it and think about it: Isn't the Bricklin story truly a New Brunswick legend? Wasn't the Bricklin an oddity? Isn't it a bit of a mystery how gullible we can be when a fast-talking huckster approaches us? It might even be considered an UFO, after all it had wings … Didn't it?

The intention of *Legends, Oddities & Mysteries … including UFO experiences in New Brunswick* is to add an extra tint to the colourful world that is New Brunswick. It's meant to be fun. Read and enjoy the stories and the great illustrations by New Brunswick artist Carol Taylor. Thanks Carol.

The flap over gull wings as New Brunswick got Brickled

There are some New Brunswick stories that are legends in themselves. The ill-fated Bricklin car is one of these. It is also a mystery to some, an oddity to others and, with its famous 'Gull Wing' doors it might even qualify as an Unidentified Flying Object ... save for the fact that the Bricklin never flew, either literally or figuratively!

The story of the Bricklin starts in the prosperous 1970s when New Brunswick had a dreamer for a Premier who was discovered by one of the all-time great dream merchants, Malcolm Bricklin; a fast-talking Texan.

The Bricklin car was certainly ahead of its time. It was like a poor man's Corvette, made of fibreglass and acrylic long before the Corvette went plastic, and its doors opened up instead of out ... that's why they called it Gull-Winged but as a hitherto unknown New Brunswick writer named Stillman Pickens said in his introduction to the book How to Brickle "ya know what a mess a seagull can make ..."

One of the big problems with the car was that the doors were unpredictable, often flying open at red lights and refusing to close again until the car was put in reverse. In addition the fancy headlights could also open and close like eyes. Unfortunately they, too, often stuck and it was not unusual to see a Bricklin cruising around

Enchanted as they were with the "gull-wing" doors New Brunswickers forgot what a mess seagulls can make!

winking at other cars.

Some people say that's what Richard Hatfield's orange Bricklin did when he drove it around the province campaigning for re-election in 1974 but people didn't catch on to what the car was trying to tell them, they re-elected the government of the man who was driving it.

On June 25, 1974, nine months after he had promised the first Bricklins would come off the assembly line, Malcolm Bricklin rented a ballroom for $50,000 at the Four Seasons Hotel at Park Avenue and Fifty-Second Street in New York. He filled it with government and bank officials, media, Bricklin dealers, car hobbyists and an assortment of well-heeled appearing men and women recommended by a pricey public relations firm.

As they jostled for a good view and another cocktail or two Malcolm Bricklin's father literally branded the pure

branding iron. Malcolm assured the gasping crowd that
because of the magic of its acrylic body the brand could
soon be buffed away.

Malcolm Bricklin and Richard Hatfield basked in
the limelight that was just the beginning of what was to
come. The two appeared on the *Today* show, the Bricklin
was featured in *Playboy* and Malcolm promised Americans 12,000 cars in the first year of operation and
100,000 cars after four years.

The car bodies for the big New York show had been
manually produced with the combination of fibreglass
and acrylic hand-molded and hand-laid. The first cars
came off the ill-equipped assembly line on July 27, 1974.

By September of the next year the New Brunswick
government had paid for the engineering and development of the Bricklin car and was paying much of the
cost of keeping the American complex in operation. It's
investment had reached $23 million.

On Sept. 27, 1975 the plant doors in Saint John's
Grandview Industrial Park closed, soon to be followed
by the plant in Minto. Clarkson Gordon Company had
finally been hired to prepare the first-ever operating
budget for the car company. Their report said the company would continue to lose money into 1976 and would
require more government money to sustain it. Two days
after they received the report, and two years after they
should have had one, the government put Bricklin
Canada Ltd. into receivership.

In all some 2,800 Bricklins were produced. It has
become an accepted fact that the first few cost more than
$50,000 to produce ... they sold for less than $7,000 in
the U.S.

There are various estimates of how much money
was actually owed by Bricklin at the time his U.S. com-

panies were declared bankrupt but Hal Fredericks' and Allan Chambers' book *Bricklin*, published by Brunswick Press in 1977 quotes the figure of $34.6 million, their tangible assets were listed at $1.6 million. Insofar as New Brunswick's investment is concerned the authors suggest the province had to borrow the $23 million invested in Bricklin on the American market, they quote bank sources as saying the province's credibility suffered as a result in financial circles.

There are still some Bricklins around New Brunswick. Most of them have become cherished additions to collectors' showrooms and there is one that calls the New Brunswick Museum 'home.' It will be on display at the Market Square site from time-to-time.

And what of Malcolm Bricklin and Richard Hatfield? The infamous Malcolm, according to a 1995 story in *The Evening Times Globe*, is still a dream merchant. At that time he had just designed a battery driven bicycle that investors were clamouring to put their money in. As Mr. Barnum so wisely said, ... *there's one born every minute.*

Richard Hatfield is now deceased but the people of New Brunswick were very forgiving ... they elected him to office twice more, having relegated the Bricklin story to their burgeoning shelf of colourful political peccadillos.

Then, in 1987, they decided after 17 years that enough was enough and threw out the entire Hatfield government. As a result, for the first time in Canadian history a political party swept into power taking every seat in the Legislature. **dd**

Holy Ghosts

A mysterious breeze
haunts this Apohaqui church

In the Village of Apohaqui, the birthplace of New Brunswick Premier Frank McKenna, there is a small Anglican Church that is nearly 125 years old at this writing. In December of 1994 a parishioner, Laura Stockdale, wrote to me to share the wonder and the mystery that surrounds the *Church of the Ascension,* whose elegant steeple towers protectively over the historic houses and prosperous farms of the surrounding area, despite the disaster that nearly gutted the landmark.

Here is her story:dd

On September 11, 1994 a freak storm hit this area, hail turned the ground white, there was thunder and lightening and the steeple on our church was struck.

The top part was blown into little pieces. The roof of the church was damaged from the lightening going out both sides under the steeple area, melting holes in the shingles. Then the falling timbers from the steeple made other holes. The electrical system was burnt out and the sound system was cooked!

Everyone was devastated to see our beautiful old landmark in such a condition.

As the old saying goes, 'Nothing is so bad but it might be worse.'

The church didn't burn and the beautiful stained

glass windows weren't even cracked. There were three fuses in the electrical panel that weren't burnt out, one ran the organ, the other two the furnace. They were okay.

The insurance company sent their appraisers and structural engineers to assess the damage. One day, my husband, along with the adjusters and some other church members picked up enough pieces of the steeple to lay on the ground and more-or-less reconstruct one side of the steeple.

They found all but a section containing about three rows of shingles.

While they were looking for that piece a gentle breeze shook the maple trees that surround the church ... and the piece they wanted fell out of one of them!

I asked my husband if he looked up in the tree to see if the Guardian Angel was sitting up there.

There must be a message for us all in this whole event. We haven't discovered what it is yet, but I'm certain we will.

Last Sunday morning the Bishop was at our church for Confirmation services. A few minutes before the service started a sort of wave started in the west end of the church and, with a lot of mild snapping and creaking went to the east end.

The structure is supposed to be sound even though the lightening did cause some movement.

My friend and I were in the choir, she looked at me, I looked at her and said, "I hope that is the Holy Spirit!"

I guess I was right.

When Bishop Lemon started his sermon he mentioned the lightening strike and said, "that is the way the Holy Spirit comes. It strikes you!"

We joke about these things but with some reservations.

Christ Church Cathedral Capers

One of New Brunswick's most famous ghosts is that of Mrs. John Medley, widow of New Brunswick's first Anglican Bishop. The story is wonderfully told in Stuart Trueman's book *Ghosts, Pirates and Treasure Trove ... The Phantoms that Haunt New Brunswick* following his interview with Hampton native Rev. David Mercer, when he was serving as assistant curate at Christ Church Cathedral in Fredericton.

The then young clergyman concurred that Mrs. Medley was indeed said to come up Church Street and enter the Cathedral by the west door, but that he really didn't know what she did after that nor, apparently did he know why the good lady (a Florence Nightingale protege) did so.

Canon Lyman Harding, in his book *Citizens with the Saints*, claims Mrs. Medley had a very strong purpose behind her haunting of the Cathedral; she despised Bishop Kingdon, her husband's successor. She is said, in fact, to have hidden or destroyed all Bishop Kingdon's correspondence with her late husband. In his turn Bishop Kingdon was not greatly enamoured of Mrs. Medley either: he nicknamed her Mrs. Proudy.

Ghosts aside, certainly the Cathedral's very architecture and the stone figure of a recumbent Bishop Medley are enough to spark the most dormant imagination

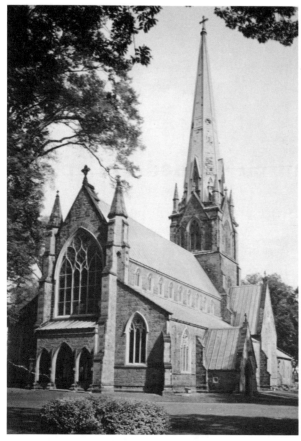

and make this magnificent edifice well worth a visit anytime.

For some as yet unknown reason Mrs. Medley was unhappy with the new Bishop who was to succeed her husband and, apparently, she has chosen to haunt Christ Church Cathedral in Fredericton ever since.

More Anglican Hauntings

The oldest Anglican rectory in New Brunswick is the Trinity Church rectory in Kingston on the Kingston Peninsula, Kings County. It was built in 1787 by the church's first resident clergyman, Rev. James Scovil of Waterbury, Connecticut, who arrived complete with family and slaves. The Scovil family actually provided the church with its rectors for the next 90 years as three generations served in that capacity. Following that the family home was turned over to the church and has continued to serve as a rectory every since.

Canon Harding served a term as rector there but he claims his family never did experience the haunting that made others nervous about entering the premises. He suggested I contact historian/writer Doris Calder.

Yes, Doris said, there were some mysteries connected with the rectory. Several years ago Harold Keirstead and another man took up some floor boards in the cellar while doing some renovating. When they dug up the ground beneath in preparation for laying a more solid footing they discovered a skull and were about to dig it up and remove it when they noted the surrounding soil had been planted at the four corners of a square with the pointed blades of four spades. By common consent they re-covered the area, skull, spades and all, and put the new footing over it. It was some time later before they gathered the courage to tell their story. To her knowledge, Doris said, no one has ever gone to the cellar and investigated further.

Local history and the experience of a local child suggest that the skeleton was the remains of a black child who was buried in the cellar in accordance with the traditions of the family's native African culture.

"Their reason is very simple," said Black historian Nick Skinner. "The custom was to bury family members under the floor of the dwelling, in that way the family would always be together."

It is said that the ghost of a black child was seen by four year-old Eric Campbell, whose family were living at the rectory for a short period between resident clergy. Eric, now a teenager, no longer has a clear memory of the incident but says maybe it was a ghost or maybe he was just dreaming. Whatever it was, what he saw was a small black figure.

Both Mr. Skinner and David Peters, who has done

extensive research into Black culture in the Maritimes, believe there is no symbolism involved in the four spades left by the body.

"If there was any symbolism involved there we would have discovered something about it by now," Mr. Peters said.

"Very simply all it means is that they were used to dig the grave and were left there to mark the site," said Mr. Skinner.

Ironically, in its earliest days Trinity Church in Kingston was the first Anglican Church in either Europe or America to have free pews, according to the presiding bishop of the time. In Kingston there was no discrimination among rich or poor, black, white or in-between, all were free to attend service and be properly seated. But Bishop John Inglis from Nova Scotia solidly berated them for this practice and the Parish of Kingston quickly and guiltily reverted to the practice of "selling" pews, lest some undesirables should cause disruptions during church service.

"At one time when I was rector at Christ Church in St. Stephen a number of people thought that church was haunted," Canon Harding said.

"Things like carpet rods in the stairs would disappear then reappear mysteriously with no one claiming any knowledge of them. The mischief was said to have been caused for the sole purpose of aggravating Archdeacon Edmond Hailstone."

The Anglican Church in Springfield, just above Fredericton was definitely the site of a haunting, Canon Harding said. When the Rev. Ed. Parkinson and his wife were preparing to fall into bed the first night after moving into the rectory Mr. Parkinson was amazed to see the former rector, the late Rev. Harry T. Buckland dressed in full church regalia of cassock, surplice and stole standing at the foot of the bed. Mr. Parkinson expressed having felt a sense of comfort from this sighting and promptly fell into a contented sleep. The next morning, to his surprise, his wife told him of her strange experience the previous night. She, too, had seen the same apparition at the foot of the bed and experienced the same sense of comfort.

Moncton's Magnetic Hill
A Magic Passageway?

No book claiming to examine New Brunswick mysteries would be considered complete until it has seriously examined the story of the Magnetic Hill near Moncton.

The first thing to be said, right up front, is that no one around here claims that magnets have anything to do with the hill. That's not to say there aren't those who believe or suspect a magnetic force is at work at the site but from the very beginning the family who owned the property made it clear.

"It's an optical illusion," they said.

No one believed them. To this day theories abound as to why at a certain location vehicles of any kind coast uphill. Even the water in the ditch beside the road runs uphill!

The Magnetic Hill has attracted other thoughtful visitors, in addition to tourists over the years, many of them of a scientific bent. One writer, Jacques Bergier, claimed that an entire Indian Village disappeared at the site.

Another writer, Nicole Taghert, the author of the book *Secret Doors of the Earth* claims the Magnetic Hill is a magic passageway to a strange hidden world created by "negative mascon." Mascon being a concentration of mass out of the ordinary with gravitational properties of its own.

**Mystery surrounds Moncton's Magnetic Hill ...
did an Indian Village really disappear here? Or is
it a magic passageway to the unknown?**

It was back in the month of June in the year 1933
when three young newspapermen, Jack Brayley (my
mother's first cousin), Stuart Trueman and John Bruce
"recognized a story but failed to recognize a fortune." [1]

The story started with an anecdote the three men,
reporters for *The Telegraph-Journal*, heard. It seems that
early in the 20th Century a clergyman was bringing children home from a picnic when it started to rain. He
stopped his touring car at the foot of a hill to put up the
side flaps but, to his amazement, the car started to coast
up the hill again all by itself. It was not moving at a
rapid pace and he was able to jump in and drive it down
the hill it had just coasted up. Fascinated, he and the
children played the game a few times before chugging
away home in a mood of wonderment.

To investigate this tale meant driving 100 miles to
Moncton over dirt roads in a 1931 roadster, no easy ex-
pedition in 1933. The three men left at three o'clock in
the morning after the paper had been 'put to bed.'

Once in the general area they spent hours trying one hill after another on the outskirts of Moncton in their search for one on which their roadster would "coast up hill." Finally at 11 a.m. to their amazement they discovered what would forever after be known to the world as the Magnetic Hill.

With great glee they returned to Saint John and their typewriters where they pounded out the first stories of what has become one of New Brunswick's most popular tourist attractions.

[1] *The complete story* Up the Down Hillside *by Stuart Trueman may be found in his book* An Intimate History of New Brunswick *and is well worth the read. dd*

The Making of Legends
on the Miramichi

According to my old *Collins Graphic Dictionary* legends started out by being chronicles of the lives of saints then, eventually, any ancient tale or unauthentic fable or family tradition could claim such status.

If such are so then I have no compunction in presenting the following *Legend of Sheephouse Brook* or its fellow *Legend of Square Forks*. Both come from what is commonly referred to as the Miramichi area of New Brunswick.

The legends were written by elementary school students but there is magic in the tales that goes beyond simple stories prompted by class assignments.

Doug Murray, now retired as school teacher and principal at Harkins Elementary School, was teaching Grade 5 in 1985.

"We were studying about myths and legends in both poetry and prose and, in the course of my teaching, I told the students about a beautiful place I had heard about from an old woodsman and eventually found. I told them about the falls, the foam on the water and how isolated the area was from civilization.

"We decided to take that spot and make up a legend about it. The kids threw ideas out and I wrote them on the board, when we finished I told them to write a story, using the different ideas we had come up with and I

Sheephouse Brook

promised them I would take the best story and put it on a board on a tree at Sheephouse Brook."

The winner of the contest was 12 year-old Lloyd Ward, a native boy from Burnt Church. Murray edited the story, had it typed and, true to his word, took the story to Sheephouse Brook and tacked it to a tree.

Here is the story as it appears today encased in plastic and hung on a tree at Sheephouse Brook ... but it is by no means the end of the story, or the legend:

The Legend of Sheephouse Brook

Long, long ago when pioneers were around in this country, there was a settler looking for a piece of land that he would live on. He looked all over the meadows, the woods and the hills. One fine day when he was looking for a place to farm he got lost. He had no weapons or ammunition with him, and having no food he started to get hungry. After going without food for three days, he started to have fainting spells.

On the fourth day the Indian god, Glooscap, saw him. He was the god of all the Indians, and he felt pity for the white man even though he didn't like people to live on his land. Glooscap wanted this land where the green grass, meadows, beautiful flowers and tall trees grew as a special garden for everyone to enjoy. So Glooscap thought of a great idea! He told the lost bewildered white man that if he helped, the man would have to give Glooscap a solemn promise.

Glooscap told him that if he did not settle or live on his land, he would lead him to safety. The man agreed with Glooscap's pact. Because the man was so hungry, Glooscap gave him some sheep to eat. At the bottom of a canyon there was a small stream and in the stream the man saw sheep drinking the cool fresh water. After killing several of the sheep for food he left their woolly hides in the brook.

Ever since that day, nobody has gone against Glooscap's wishes and the land in that country remains unsettled and unspoiled. Everyone is allowed to visit Glooscap's garden to cut wood, fish, hunt or just visit but no one lives there.

As a sign of faith between Glooscap and his new friend, he makes the water produce piles of foam around the rocks and sticks in the brook. If you should visit the area around Sheephouse Brook in the Miramichi country you will still find the land as it was first made by Glooscap. In addition you will also be able to see the sheep hides in the brook and be reminded of Glooscap's good deed!

The area around Sheephouse Brook was, and is, forest land owned by Repap but reserved by the company as part of its 25 year forest management plan. In 1989 Joe O'Neill, Repap's vice-president of woodlands learned of the "legend" created in Doug Murray's classroom and later posted on a tree at the site.

This had a major influence on the company's decision to develop the area as a park. In the process of creating the park they harvested over mature patches of timber and planted new trees.

Some workers two kilometres upstream from the falls made an astounding find one day as they were clearing some of the old trees. It was an Indian arrowhead and, archaeologists in Ottawa told them, it was 2,000 years old and made by the Hopewell Indian tribe in Ohio. Proof, the archaeologists said, that the Micmacs must have been trading with other Indians over great distances.

Magic?

You bet. But that's not the end of the story.

In Joe O'Neill's office hangs a picture of Sheephouse Falls taken by a man named Tom Kingston, who was alone in the area at the time. When his film was developed a mysterious man wearing a red cap and blue jeans can be seen kneeling behind the falls, washing something in the foaming water.

A sheepskin, maybe?

✳✳✳✳

In anticipation of an area called Square Forks being developed, as another natural treasure of the area, Douglas Murray had students in the 1988 class at Harkins Elementary School write a legend for that area.

The winner was 11 year-old Jennifer Ward, a native student from Eel Ground. Here is Jennifer's story:

The Legend of Square Forks

Many moons ago there was a beautiful river lined with rustling grasses and many-coloured flowers that scented the land with the smell of perfume. Tall evergreens towered along its banks and the surrounding countryside was alive with animals, birds and fish.

Dark One detested this wonderland of nature and decided to destroy the beauty of the river. He threw huge boulders into the centre of the river until eventually it came apart. The river flowed in two different directions and its beauty was only half of what it was before. Dark One hid the rivers in deep dark canyons and the beauty of the country withered and died.

The flowers faded, the beautiful trees shed their leaves, and the animals and fish quietly left the desolate land.

The two new rivers flowed lonely and sad for many years until Glooscap took pity on them. He used his power of goodness to make a channel that joined the two lonely rivers together. The rivers rushed to meet each other and together they had enough power to overcome the evil magic of the Dark One and carved a new course of their own.

Dark One got so angry because his plan was ruined that he stomped his foot in the water like an angry child. The heel of his foot formed a waterfall and his toes created a set of rapids in the river.

When the two rivers joined, their beauty returned as never before. The water laughingly danced over the rocks, flowers again scented the air and the trees painted the countryside in beautiful greens, yellows and reds. The creatures of the forest returned to live happily along the river and the fish once again jumped playfully in the dark deep pools of water.

Today you can go to Square Forks and see the place where the two rivers meet and high canyon walls where Dark One tried to hide them. To remind us how evil Dark One was, you can still see the waterfall formed by his heel and downstream, a small set of rapids formed by the toes of his foot.

The mystery of the
seagoing skull

Around June 19-20,1959, 34 fishermen from the village of Escuminac drowned in a freak and unexpected storm leaving a legacy of grief in the community. A wind-sanded stark memorial still weathers the storm, looking out to sea for the men whose sudden disappearance left this community virtually bereft of fathers, sons and husbands.

More than 35 years later, on June 2, 1995, Aquila Manuel, a new generation of Escuminac fishermen, was enjoying a morning lunch on his fishing boat when a stark, human skull surfaced beside the boat and he found himself returning the stare of its socketless eyes.

"Four of us saw it," he said and described the sight that met the lobstermen who had just finished working their lobster traps in the shallow, five meter deep area of crystal clear water.

"It was a human skull for sure. Two eyes and a big hole where the nose should be, very white, bright but the jaw was missing.

"But it was a human skull. It was looking up at me. It was so, so white ... as white as a skull!"

Manuel called the RCMP and a dive team, along with officers from the Department of Fisheries and Oceans searched the outer limits at the bottom of Miramichi Bay near the Northumberland Strait, work-

Strong winds could roll a skull along the ocean bottom like a soccer ball, or a tumbleweed on the prairie, according to DOF personnel.

ing their way through the lobster traps in a systematic underwater grid pattern without luck.

There is a strong feeling among the fishermen of the area that the skull may belong to one of those tragic fishermen lost in 1959. But whose skull was it? And why did it surface that particular day then disappear?

Strong winds were suggested as the reason for the skull's appearance. These winds have been known to blow buoys and 70 lb. lobster traps onto the beach. According to Department of Fisheries personnel, on hand for the search, the skull "would have rolled along the ocean bottom like a soccer ball, or a tumbleweed on the prairie."

Strong winds are no rarity in these waters off the New Brunswick coast but this is the first time they have been blamed for bringing a human skull to the surface on a clear, calm day.

RCMP spokesman Cpl. Dan Lessard believes the remains are probably still down there, beneath the ocean, waiting to be found someday but the skull, he said, could be anywhere by now.dd

The Fastest Ship in All the World

And her name was Marco Polo ...

That's the theme of the musical suite written for this Saint John wonder ship, launched April 17, 1851. Those were the days of *Wooden Ships and Iron Men* and the City of Saint John was at its most magnificent stage of development.

Relegated for many years to naval history books the Marco Polo recently has come into its own, thanks largely to the efforts of high school teacher Barry Ogden.

Ogden maintains that in reality the Marco Polo is Canada's most famous vessel, despite the Bluenose dime to the contrary.

Certainly in terms of naval knowledge Ogden is probably right. Even Australians honour the vessel with an annual wingding to commemorate their ancestors who sailed to Australia on the "fastest ship in all the world" during her heyday.

There are many who maintain that the Marco Polo's accident of birth was responsible for her great speed. Hers was one of the largest hulls ever built in a Canadian yard at the time, combining as it did the underwater shape of a clipper and the amidship girth of a cargo carrier. Perhaps it was this monster hull that, on the April day as she slid from the slip in Saint John, caused her prow to become buried deep in the mud and sludge

... and they called her Marco Polo!

of the harbour bottom, twisting the keel into what mariners maintained was a crippling flaw for it hogged in the centre six inches higher than at the bow and stern.

Salvaged by her owners she embarked on her maiden voyage and immediately showed her stern to all competitors by crossing the Atlantic to Liverpool, laden with timber, in just 15 days.

On July 4, 1852 she took off for Melbourne Australia with 930 passengers and 60 crew and, flying before gale winds, she reached Melbourne in a mere seventy-six days ...the previous best time had been considered to be 100 days.

Just to prove it was no fluke she set sail from Melbourne for Liverpool and matched her previous time to the day!

In just five months and twenty-one days, seventeen of which she had spent in Australia, the Marco Polo had circumnavigated the world and was proclaimed to be "the fastest ship in all the world."

For 15 years she plied the seas and no other ship could ever touch her time. Although time worn by 1867 she still was able to make the trip between Melbourne and Liverpool in seventy-six days, a time no other vessel, sail or steam had been able to match.

In her early days she was decked out as a fashionable and luxurious passenger ship with maple panelling, crimson velvet upholstery, stained glass doors and circular glass hatch lights and capable of carrying 1,000 passengers. By the 1880s, still fast in her work, she had become a tramp steamer and was carrying a load of timber in July of 1883 when a young girl named Lucy Maude Montgomery (of Anne of Green Gables fame) watched as, caught in a summer gale, she drove toward the shore of Cavendish, Prince Edward Island "coming before the gale with every stitch of canvas set ... a sight never to be forgotten."

She struck bottom 300 yards out and keeled over. Although the crew was set to abandon her the people of Cavendish held up a hand-lettered sign telling them to stick to the ship because the sea was so treacherous.

Despite the fact that she was broached and waves were breaking over her the Marco Polo held together through the night and, in the morning, a boat put out from shore and rescued the entire crew.

Lucy Maude Montgomery was one of the many Prince Edward Islanders who watched the spectacle. Her essay on the wrecking of the Marco Polo won the first prize in an essay contest in the *Montreal Witness* .

Someday Barry Ogden and his fellow supporters of the Marco Polo Project hope to build a replica of the famous ship and sail it once again for all the world to see.dd

Stories from St. Martins

Family Fun

Like many New Brunswick villages, the Village of St. Martins is filled with stories, stories of the feats of sea captains and fishermen and of the days when it was a thriving shipbuilding community. Stories of people.

My New Brunswick roots, through my grandmother, Caroline Tufts (Ryder), run deep in the history of this colourful community. For this reason it was important to me to include a St. Martins story or two in this book and that was when I remembered *Letters to Patricia*, a book my father wrote to my homesick sister (Pat [Ryder] McLeod of Fredericton) when she was working in Ottawa many long years ago.

These humorous letters were a delight not just to our family but to all those with whom they were shared. However, a word of explanation is in order.

My father, Kenneth Ryder, had little tolerance for people who put on airs and his letters reflect this. He writes under the name "Aunt Clarissa" and the letters are his attempt to bring an elderly aunt, who he felt had lost touch with her roots and become a bit of a snob, down to earth as it were.

Here then is one of the wild and wonderful tales in *Letters to Patricia* written by Ken Ryder in 1957.

Saint John, N.B.
15 January 1957

Miss Patricia Ryder,
Ottawa

Dear Niece Patricia:
    Having completed my household chores for the morning, I thought I would drop you a line, hoping to find you in good health.
    Having heard so much of your wonderful relatives on your mother's side (Phillip LORD Wharton, Uncle Frank, et al) I think it is high time someone spoke up for your father's relatives. I shall give them to you slowly, one each letter, so that you will not become too excited, or nauseated.
    One of your best known relatives on your dear father's side was his Cousin Oedipus, son of your paternal grandmother's sister. Their home was in Quaco (as it is so fondly remembered by we historians) to ordinary run-of-the-mill people it is known as St. Martins.
    Cousin Oedipus' mother, dear, sweet, Freelove, was a very romantic and sentimental girl who loved and sang all the love songs of her day (what a day!) and, in confidence she told me that she chose your second-cousin Oedipus' name from one of these songs. I think you will recall it ... Oedipus the Ocean – Ohio's the Sky ... Remember? The least said about Oedipus' father the better, as a matter of fact very little can be said of him as he just stopped over in Quaco for about an hour one day and has never been seen since! It was undoubtedly love at first (and last) sight.
    Even when Oedipus was a small boy he gave every indication of being an unusual character, even his appearance was unusual. As his mother was very poor it was necessary for Oedipus to make do with anything in the

line of wearing apparel that came to hand. Under these circumstances it was not unusual to see Oedipus careering down the road in his goat-cart looking like a Roman charioteer with two scrawny arms sticking through an oat sack and his beautiful pointed head proudly erect.

Inevitably Oedipus grew to manhood, if anything his head was more pointed than ever, or it could be that it was more pronounced on his scrawny six-feet, eleven inch form. However, this did not interfere with his becoming an outstanding athlete in Quaco and district. He was unfortunate though in playing hockey; if he happened to be checked into the boards he would invariably plunge head-first and his head would drive right through. The games were usually held up ten to fifteen minutes to extricate him. This led to him being expelled from hockey.

There are so many things I could tell you about Oedipus but time is running short and his contemporaries in Quaco will talk about him for hours, if given an opportunity.

Out on the south shore of Quaco, when the tide is low, an observant person can see, spelled in seaweed the name Oedipus. This is the memorial of the people of Quaco to your second cousin.

I have merely told you this so that you can be proud of your dear father's relatives. Next time, I will tell you about his Cousin Airwick.

Your loving Aunt,
Clarissa

Nancy Sears' stories

Whenever possible I like to share "first told" tales with my readers. To this end, I called Nancy Sears (who I can proudly call kin) and asked for her help. She obliged with two possibly related stories. She shares these stories with the many people who, while visiting St. Martins, spend some of their time with Nancy, chief guide and proud owner of *Fundy Hiking and Nature Tours.*

Nancy said her stories have been handed down through her grandmother and on to her own children for nine generations now. She also suggested that I give Aynsley Brown a call with the thought that perhaps he could add something to her tales. I did, and he did, and here are the stories.

The mystery of the
Fletcher family from Orange Hill

The first part of this double-barrelled story started with Nancy's great-great grandfather who used to cut hay on Berry's Beach Marsh with his father.

He told Nancy that one day, it would have been around the mid-1800s, a boat sailed up the bay and dropped anchor then let down a rowboat. The rowboat came through the marsh and two rough-looking characters, one rowing the boat the other carrying something like a small casket, asked the brothers if they knew where there was a rise of land with three large pine trees on it.

The brothers said they didn't know of any land where there would be three large pine trees because all the biggest trees had been cut down long before to build the masts for ships.

"The row boat went back through the marsh again and the men and the sail boat disappeared. My great-great-grandfather and his brother could never decide whether they were real people or ghosts. They said they were rough-looking enough to be pirates and they assumed that's what they were ... but whether they were real pirates or ghost pirates they never knew for sure."

When Nancy was growing up her grandmother continued the family's storytelling tradition and one of these involved a mystery family that intrigued St. Martins residents early in the 20th Century.

Was it pirate's gold that made the Fletcher family rich? After they died no one knows where the money went nor, for that matter, where it came from in the first place.

The family's name was "Fletcher" and there were three of them, two bachelor brothers and a spinster sister, who lived at Orange Hill, their names were Will, Bill and Ida, as close as she can remember.

"They were what was always called 'dirt poor' because their only source of income was a few chickens they kept and every day Ida would come down the hill with a basket of eggs to sell in the village. She would make her purchases and trudge back up the hill and through the woods to their shack.

"Then one day they came down the hill, all three of

them, and walked into the village and bought a house right there in the middle of St. Martins. And they paid for it in gold!

"From then on about once a month, Nancy's grandfather would hitch up the family horse and buggy and drive one of the brothers to Saint John where he would drop him off at a specific corner each time, under orders to leave and not come back until a certain designated hour.

"When he left St. Martins the brother did not have any money but always assured my grandfather he would be paid before the return trip. And every time my grandfather would pick him up at the specified time he would have money for the return trip.

"Eventually, all three of them died and to this day no one knows where their sudden riches came from and no one knows who inherited the wealth after the last Fletcher was gone."

Rumour has it that they found gold in the field around their shack up on Orange Hill. The question that still lingers is: Was it Orange Hill that the pirates Nancy's great-grandfather talked to back in the mid-1800s were looking for? Had there once been three tall pine trees there?

Aynesly Brown said when he was young he heard stories about how the Fletchers used to go out at night digging for riches.

"As the story goes they found some out on a little island to the left of the marshes. Yet I once saw a hole in the ground near their house that had been dug during the night one time when I was out deer hunting. And there was a crooked pipe left there. I can't say for sure whose pipe it was but neither the pipe or the hole had been there in the field when I was there the day before.

"Of course some people claimed they saw the

Fletchers with old coins but I don't know if anyone really did."

All that anyone knows for sure is that the Fletchers were always 'dirt poor' then suddenly were rich enough to buy a house in the village.

Nancy said "one fascinating mystery still remains unsolved there on the hill where the old Fletcher place used to be. A beautiful field of cultivated lily-of-the-valley is growing wild there and it's the only place in St. Martins that I know of where you can find it. When I take my people hiking up through the area I always show them the field and tell them the story of the Fletchers and their instant riches." *dd*

Major Studholm's buried treasure and the iron box of Belleisle

... one, two or three Kings County mysteries?

Even before I moved to Hampton I had heard the story of Major Gilford Studholm's treasure. The way I heard it was that in fairly recent history ... sometime in the 1930s maybe ... a family that was living on the Studholm farm at Apohaqui suddenly struck it very rich. It was said that, in the process of building the foundation for a new barn, they had come upon a chest filled with gold ... and lived happily ever after off the interest.

Then, over the years, other stories of the Studholm treasure surfaced. These stories were intertwined with those of the buried treasure said to have been found in or near Belleisle Bay. In truth, they could still be Studholm-related. Although the farm is located on the Kennebecasis River at Apohaqui, there was also the Studholm mansion (*Grantery Hall?*), which no one seems quite able to locate.

Was it, perhaps, a few miles from Apohaqui on Belleisle Bay?

According to one story, when Major Studholm died in 1792 at his rural retreat, where the Millstream enters the Kennebecasis near Apohaqui his locked iron box, said to contain gold coins, was found open. Its contents, along with a metal pot from the kitchen, were missing.

Major Studholm was duly buried on the hillside above his home but, over the years, people continued to speculate on the whereabouts of the missing gold.

An article in the Saint John *Weekly Sun* of Dec. 12, 1894 noted that three strangers arrived in Saint John one day in 1888 and, after recruiting the help of a local diviner, went to Major Studholm's grave site where they set the divining mechanism in motion.

The rod led them further down the hill to an adjoining field which nurtured a solitary pine tree. The divining rod became strongly attracted to the base of the tree and the men began digging.

They carefully followed the required ritual for such occasions first inscribing a large circle around the tree then placing an open Bible on the ground inside the ring, to placate the spirit of those dead who still retained an interest in the treasure.

The standard rules demand that once the digging has begun no word must be spoken and no soil from the hole may be placed outside the ring.

It wasn't too long before they struck something hard and, hearts in their throats, they began to dig more feverishly around the obstacle. But the obstacle was so large it seemed to have no perimeter and one of the men became so discouraged he blurted out the words, "I don't believe it's there at all!"

Of course the spell was broken, the divining rod went limp and gave no further indication of gold or metal to be found in the area.

But the third story, a Maliseet Legend, had a more upbeat ending. Unfortunately not for the Maliseet Indian involved!

Interestingly enough it involves the same three American travellers within the same time frame as quoted in the story in the *Weekly Sun* .

The story has been handed down in the Paul family from Noel Paul, the founder of the Maliseet Indian

Woodstock Reserve. It tells of Noel Paul and a number of other Indians being camped in the Millidgeville area on The Brothers islands when they were approached by some strangers in a boat.

The leader of the men approached Noel Paul and said he had been looking for him because he had dreamed about him the previous fall. In the dream Paul had told him where to find buried treasure.

Before returning to his boat the stranger asked Paul where he would dig to look for gold. As a joke Paul decided to take the stranger to the highest point on the southern end of the island on his return. He showed him a spot clear of undergrowth and said that was where he would dig.

The stranger thanked him, cut down a small bush and peeled the bark from it before sticking it into the ground indicated by Paul. They then returned, Paul to the encampment the stranger to his boat.

The next morning the stranger's boat was gone and that afternoon some of the Paul children discovered a freshly dug hole about four or five feet deep in the spot where the peeled bush had been standing. Further investigation indicated that some heavy rectangular object had been pulled out and the land closest to Belleisle Bay had caved in. There were signs that something heavy had been dragged down the slope to the water.

When Noel Paul inspected the site more closely he discovered a triangular shaped gold coin placed on a flat rock nearby.

He accepted the coin as his reward for leading the man to the gold.

As in all legends variety adds spice to the story and the legend of the Studholm gold has variety to spare.

According to the Maliseet story the timing of that event was close to 1875 but it is generally believed that the fortune seekers were looking for the Studholm treasure.

Yet the facts, if they are so, indicate that it was 1888 when the strangers sailed into Belleisle Bay in their quest for gold and it was June 11, 1888, according to customs records of the time, when gold coin to the value of $13,000 was sent from Saint John by Celeb S. Stokes, a sea captain's son from Massachusetts.

The story goes that the *Susan*, a woodboat hired by Stokes, sailed upriver and into Belleisle Bay where they dropped anchor. They were presumed to be American tourists out for a cruise and their sporadic stops and starts were attributed to the party nature of the voyage.

Early one morning a farmer watched as the trio from the *Susan* took measurements along the shore. They then selected a large flat stone on which they perched a tripod. After it was adjusted to their satisfaction two of the men returned to the boat and Stokes, described as being a "tall, thin man wearing a long linen duster and a straw hat," was left on shore.

The crew then placed the *Susan* into a position dictated by the man on shore and again dropped anchor and the punt picked up Stokes and the tripod.

Once back on the boat they began probing the shallow bottom with a long, steel rod. Apparently the rod hit something hard and one of the men jumped overboard, completely clothed, and dived under water. He came up with a large iron box and the jubilant crew set sail for Saint John.

The link to Major Studholm was determined when Stokes told the writer of the *Weekly Sun* article about his father, a sea captain, who was wrecked at sea in 1848 and cast ashore in Korea. While there he became acquainted with an old, English speaking hermit. The hermit hid his treasures in a room he had dug out beneath his cabin. Among his treasures was a map which revealed the location of the Studholm treasure on Belleisle Bay. The hermit died and Stokes took the charts and, after escaping from Korea to Hong Kong, was able to bring them home to Massachusetts in 1887. The following year his son and two other men went to Belleisle Bay in search of the treasure.

Which of the above stories is closest to the truth of what happened?

Was it Major Studholm's treasure that was found and shipped to the United States by Stokes in 1888?

Did Stokes find it in Belleisle Bay?

Or was it Stokes whose divining attempts were thwarted at Apohaqui?

Or did some lucky person living on the Studholm farm find the missing gold?

Or is the gold still missing?

Who knows? dd

Kingston's Lunar Rogue
and Mysterious Stranger

Since there really is 'nothing new under the sun,' it is amazing how in this day and age we can all be so easily duped from time-to-time.

Take jail escapees, for example. In fact take one of New Brunswick's most famous escapees of recent years, Allan Legere. Should anyone wonder how he became so clever about tricking his captors, one need only remember that Mr. Legere had lots of time to read and learn as he languished in one cell or another throughout most of his life.

Quite possibly the stories of Henry More Smith ... alias Henry Frederic Moon, alias William Newman, aliases so on and so forth as needed, were among his readings.

Smith is this province's all-time most famous escape artist. Doris Calder calls him *The Mysterious Stranger* in her book *All Our Born Days,* and Barbara Grantmyre refers to him as the *Lunar Rogue* in her book of the same name.

Without doubt the legends surrounding the life of this rogue are among New Brunswick's best. I highly recommend reading both books for their entertainment value as well as for the practical value they may have for today's modern rogue.

Barbara Grantmyre's book starts out:

***Using straw from his mattress, bits of rag and
his own blood he created a family of puppets and
entertained all who would listen.***

"On the eve of May 4th, 1815, a man loaded with
chains lay in a dark, dank cell in Kingston Gaol, Kingston, New Brunswick. The next day he was to be tried
for his life.

"He was a liar, a cheat and a thief. He had charm
but no warmth of heart, remarkable powers but little
common sense. He had a craving for mischief ..."

A more apt description of Henry More Smith could
not be written.

Ms. Grantmyre's guide as she follows Smith in and
out of one gaol after another, while he cheats and steals
his way from Canada to the United States and back again,

is a small book written by Smith's gaoler Walter Bates, at one time the High Sheriff of Kings County.

While jailed at Kingston (the first time) Smith managed to fake illness so well that the Anglican priest sat death watch for him and the priest's wife sent a feather mattress for him to die on. Then while the Sheriff, the Priest the gaoler and the entire community mourned his passing Smith stole away in the night, taking to hand anything lying about or easily freed from its place along his route.

Most of the village were so convinced he had died that when, in broad daylight, one man literally saw him running away he was certain that he had seen Smith's ghost ... not Smith himself!

Smith was quick and agile, charming and ruthless as he lied and cheated to avoid his hunters. At one time he told a suspicious passerby that he was not Smith but was actually part of the search party looking for Smith!

Eventually he was caught. He was always caught, eventually. It was almost as if he had tired of the game and wanted to rest for awhile. He was returned to Kingston (on several occasions) to await his latest sentence.

On one of these occasions he carved a family of puppets and entertained all who would listen, and many did. It was difficult for most people to believe him to be as evil as Sheriff Bates maintained he was.

He was so good at getting out of chains that one can't help but wonder if the great Houdini might have taken lessons from him. It was not unusual for him to be chained in a prison cell one minute and to be free on the road the next, the chains lying limp on the floor behind the locked cell door.

One time he was brought before the Supreme Court in Fredericton and the judge asked him if he was the man named Smith who escaped from the Kingston Gaol.

He answered, "Yes."

The judge then asked, "How did you do it?"

And Smith replied, "The gaoler opened the door and the priest prayed me out."

Once returned to Kingston he began to act insane, howling and screaming and regularly breaking his chains. When led into court he continued to act the madman but refused to enter a plea and remained mute. A special jury decided he was mute due to the visitation of God. He was then sentenced to death without the benefit of clergy and placed on a diet of bread and water to await the hangman.

It was at this time that he created a family of ten puppets from the straw of his bed and his own blood. Their performances became famous throughout both Canada and the United States and people came for miles to watch the puppets perform, often paying him well for the privilege.

Smith then took up fortune telling and accurately predicted his own pardon and release.

His later exploits throughout the United States and "Upper Canada" were chronicled by Sheriff Bates until he lost track of Smith. Last reports of him came from a penitentiary in Upper Canada in 1836. **dd**

Was Brigham Young born in New Brunswick?

Just where the legend that Brigham Young was born in New Brunswick got its start is impossible to say, nor is it possible to verify. The legend, however, is solidly embedded in the memories of many families at Young's Cove and White's Cove, farming communities near the TransCanada Highway at Grand Lake.

When I first heard the oral legend I asked a friend, who is an adherent of the Church of Jesus Christ of Latter Day Saints (more commonly known as Mormons) whether the church acknowledged some grain of truth might exist in the story. He obliged me by contacting the mother church in Salt Lake City and asking for some verification of Brigham Young's birth place. The church replied in due course confirming that their records were emphatic, that Brigham Young, the man who led the founders of the Mormon religion across half a continent was born in Whittingham, Vermont in 1801.

Yet the rumours persist, as do stories handed down from generation to generation that chronicle his early life at Young's Cove.

Brigham Young, the grandson of Abraham Young a Dutch blacksmith and Loyalist after whom Young's Cove is named, was born in 1801 at his grandfather's farm and baptised in Gagetown. His mother was Catherine MacLean Young.

Although no church records have ever been found to confirm this, numerous elderly residents of the area tell the oral history of Brigham Young of Youngs Cove, who they maintain was the same man who founded the Mormon Church.

Early stories chronicle a difficult life in the area, a life where, for many, simply existing was a constant struggle. Like others before him Abraham eventually left his wife and family on the farm and went to seek a better and easier way of life in the New England states, the area from which many of the settlers in the Grand Lake area had fled as Loyalists in 1783. Unlike most of the other men who left families behind to seek their fortune Abraham was never heard of again. His family, among them a son named Brigham, existed by gradually selling the meagre stock left on the farm and through the kindness of neighbours, most of whom were little better off than they.

Abraham was rumoured to have been seen in either Vermont or New Hampshire. When his son Brigham was around 12 or 13 years of age he, too, was bit by the wanderlust. One winter day, clutching the few pennies his mother had given him to purchase some flour at the general store, he walked past the store and disappeared into the storm never to be seen again in the area around Grand Lake.

In April of 1953 the *Fredericton Gleaner* quoted people such as Mrs. Fred Nevers of the Lower Jemseg area, nearly 90 years old at the time, as confirming the truth of the story. The article was written as a follow-up to a paper by Dr. K.A. Baird published in the *Dalhousie Review*.

"Sure, he was born here," Mrs. Nevers told the newspaper. "I well remember the old folk talking abut Brigham Young and how he was a big man in the Mormon church. I guess he was a smart man but they didn't think much of the system of every man having a lot of wives." dd

Philatelists take note

New Brunswick is not without its colourful characters and one of these was Charles Connell a lumberman, magistrate and politician from Carleton County.

His father, Charles Connell was a Connecticut Loyalist which makes young Charles' most memorable endeavour even more amusing.

As a general businessman Charles made his home in Woodstock where he took an active interest in local affairs. He was a Justice of the Peace for many years, before taking on a political career in 1846, and was appointed to the Legislative Council in 1849. He resigned in 1851 and was elected as a member of the "Lower House." (These were pre-Confederation times.)

And then came the year 1858 and his appointment to the post of Postmaster General, a position which he took to heart. In fact, so dedicated was he and so confirmed in the importance of his position that when a new issue of stamps was needed in 1859 he got carried away with the assignment.

The New Brunswick Legislature decided to abandon the British system of currency and adopt the decimal system. In conformity with this it was necessary to secure postage stamps of the denomination of one, five, ten and twelve-and-a-half cents. Connell was author-

***There are those in the Woodstock area who
maintain that Charles Connell had a perfect right
to put his own likeness on the five cent stamp ...***

ized to procure them *and the details were left to his judgement.*

He proceeded to New York where he met with the American Bank Note Company and brought home a quote for the making of the plates and the printing of the stamps. The design for the one cent was to be a wood burning locomotive to mark the province's entry into an extensive railway program. The ten cent stamp was to be a likeness of the Queen made at her coronation. The twelve-and-a -half cent was of an ocean-going steamship.

In addition he ordered* a seventeen cent stamp bearing the likeness of the Prince of Wales as a boy, in Highland costume.

It was the five cent stamp that caused the furore. It bore the likeness of the Postmaster General himself, none other than Charles H. Connell.

The members of council were appalled at the thought that a commoner would put his own likeness on the stamp of a Crown colony!

It was a scandal.

The telegraph lines hummed between Connell in Woodstock and Samuel Leonard Tilley (later to become Sir Leonard Tilley and a Father of Confederation) in St. John. Throughout all this hectic correspondence it was apparent, as the late George Frederick Clarke points out in an *Atlantic Advocate* article in November of 1963, that Connell had no idea that it was the fact of his likeness on the stamp that was causing the fuss. He thought his authority to have the stamps designed and printed that was being questioned and kept replying that *the details were left to his judgement.*

On May 8, 1860 the blow fell. The Legislative Council gave its permission for the one, ten and twelve-and-one-half cent stamps to be distributed but ordered a five cent postage stamp to be struck in the likeness of the Queen which would replace the Connell stamp.

Connell resigned all his posts on May 17. Charges and countercharges ensued. Later he reimbursed the government for the costs of having the plate made and the printing done for the five cent stamp and took the offending objects home with him.

The stamps were ordered destroyed and, with the exception of one or two here and there and sheets sent to his children, they were. Later those belonging to his children were believed destroyed as well.

Connell was subsequently defeated in the election of 1861 but New Brunswickers are a forgiving lot and he was returned to the assembly in 1864 and continued being elected in subsequent elections, even to gaining a seat representing all of Carleton County, by acclamation no less, in the new Dominion government of 1867

(Confederation).

He remained a member of Parliament until his death in 1873.

And the Connell Stamp?

A sidebar here worth noting. In his story in the *Atlantic Advocate* Clarke tells of, years later, making a deal with the executors of the estate of Connell's family descendants for a birch bark canoe which had captured his imagination forty years earlier. The deal was that Clarke could have the birch bark canoe, a second canoe and the contents of the shed they were in for fifty dollars, provided he cleaned out the stuff that covered the floors.

The place was filled with various collectibles and became a treasure trove for Clarke. He found the biggest treasure of all when he scoured the place for the handle of a silver teapot he had found. It was then that he discovered a perfect pair of the Connell stamps.

He sold the stamps for around $1,000 which he then invested in oil stocks delighted, at the time of writing the article, to report that his stocks were worth $3,900 while the book value of the stamps were only $2,100. He did note that presumably the stamps would increase in value ... and they have. The catalogue price for one Connell stamp, in mint condition in 1995 was $7,500.dd

The face etched in the oven at 31 Leinster Street

When Saint John Chef David Peters operated the nationally acclaimed *Duke of Leinster* restaurant in 1975 he, and many of his patrons, were intrigued with the historic aspects of the house over which he presided.

To Peters' knowledge it was the John Roop house at 31 Leinster Street, constructed in 1777, although tenders were called for it by Andrew J. Armstrong in the *Daily Telegraph* of March 20, 1878 at which time the existing structure was presumably rebuilt over the original foundation.

"It was this foundation that attracted one of my customers who had come here from the United States.

"She read about us in *Where to Eat in Canada* and, although the cuisine interested her, it was the cellar she really came here for. Apparently many people who have a special interest in architecture make it a point to focus on the cellars and roofs of old buildings.

"Of course I agreed to let her into the cellar with her camera and she took a number of pictures, among them one of what I thought at the time was an old bake oven. It never occurred to me it was anything else, bake ovens were common items found in the cellars of houses around Saint John. Why would anyone dream it could be anything other than that? Anything so grisly as what it was.

"The woman thought there was something different

To their amazement researchers from the New Brunswick Museum discovered it was not unusual for well-to-do families to have their own crematoria in their cellars.

about it and she opened the oven door to show the unique design as well as the fine ash that still remained under the grate. When I looked at the picture of the oven I was intrigued.

" 'Isn't that strange,' I said. 'Look at the way the rust and ash has formed a picture on the door.'

"It looked for all the world like the picture of a child, the face including the bangs of her hair even her eyelashes were as clear as they could be.

"By this time the woman was getting quite hyper about it and I told her to let us clean off the door and then she could take another picture. So we picked up two burlap bags and scrubbed at the rust on the door and cleaned it right down to the clear black iron.

"This time when she took the picture it was as if the black iron door had created a negative image and the outline of the face and features were clearer and sharper than ever."

After the woman left David called the museum and, between them, they traced the history of the house and the times. To their amazement they discovered that it was not unusual for well-to-do families to have their own crematoria in their cellars and that it was a normal practice, particularly with a sickly child, for the family to cremate that child immediately after death.

Further research turned up the information that the Roop family did indeed have a sickly child who had died at a young age. Local wisdom presumes that the intense heat and light of the crematorium acted like a lens and etched the child's face in the door of her tomb.

The door was subsequently removed from the oven and is now among the collections of local historic artifacts at the New Brunswick Museum in Saint John.

Various architectural examples of the Armstrong construction were rescued from the site before the entire building was demolished in 1987.

Here is the description of the iron door as it is filed in the museum's archives:

130cm. h x 68 cm. l.

Rounded at top, has door handle at right, hinges at left. Plain au verso. Original covering appears to have been a milk white paint but there is little of this left. Surface rust covers almost the whole of the area of the door and has gone beneath surface at bottom right to eat away a section measuring 42 cm. l x max. depth of 7 cm. dd

The Great Submarine Chase of 1914 in the Bay of Fundy

This wonderful story was told by the late Jean Sweet in the February, 1972 issue of the Atlantic Advocate. It is retold here through the kind permission of her son, Ian Sweet. Thanks Binker!

Jean Sweet was one of those women well ahead of her time. She was a writer of plays, short stories and co-author of a history book still used in the school system today. For many years she was the only woman staff reporter at *The Evening Times Globe* but, before any of these activities she was a school teacher in the 1930s. Her classroom was on Partridge Island at a time when it was still a community, housing the port quarantine station and a lighthouse keeper and family.

Jean did not live on Partridge Island, she commuted to her classes five days a week on a launch, owned by the federal department of health and used to take the doctor, supplies and mail to the government staff on the island ... and to bring islanders to the city for shopping, church and so on.

The SALUCAN (translation Health of Canada) was under the command of Captain George Kinghorn and it was he who told her the following story.

Before captaining the SALUCAN he had served his sea-time first under sail on the Newfoundland fishing banks and later on the tug *Neptune*, which he claimed was the biggest and strongest in the harbour at the time of his story.

It was early in the Great War, he said, when he was serving as mate on the Neptune when, one day at noon hour, "the navy arrived!"

When the war started, he said, the Canadian Navy amounted to a couple of little old ships, one of which was in the Saint John Dry Dock for a refit at the time of this story.

"I was on deck," he said, "when the three of them arrived. A young fella, a junior officer pink-cheeked and wild-eyed running down the jetty with two seamen, armed with rifles.

"He come up to the cap of the wharf, all out of breath and shouted, 'Are you the Captain of this boat?' I told him I was mate and he asked if I could take her out alone. I said I could."

With that the rosy-cheeked officer yelled to his men, "Follow me!" and they climbed aboard the tug.

"I'm commandeering this boat in the King's name!" Pink-cheeks said. "There's a German submarine in the Bay and we're going out to look for her!"

Captain Kinghorn said he didn't know at that point whether to laugh or cry!

"Imagine a tug boat with a couple of rifles hunting for a submarine!"

The young officer stationed one man on the roof of the wheelhouse with his rifle ready and the other one on deck and then proceeded to walk the deck, his head swivelling in all directions, his eyes peeled for anything afloat or submerged.

Using a big megaphone he ordered all small craft ashore, yelling, "Get out of there! Get ashore! There's a German submarine around here – get your lines up and get ashore!"

The tugboat Neptune cruised the bay, in and out of small coves, anywhere a small vessel might be found with Pink-cheeks commanding them out of the Bay and the line of submarine fire.

In the late afternoon the Digby ferry was on its way to Saint John and Pink-cheeks ordered the Neptune to close in on her. He then hailed the bridge:

"Put on full steam ahead and steer a zig-zag course ..." he commanded. A difficult order for any seaman to carry out!

The last man hailed before dark was an old fellow putting out a net. Pink-cheeks yelled, "Get that net out of there and get ashore! There's a German submarine in the Bay!"

The old man just looked up and said, "Submarine, eh? I'll fix him, if I get him in this net," and continued with what he was doing.

"What good is that net?" Pink-cheeks hollered. "Get it up and get out of here!"

The fisherman straightened up and looked him in the eye, insulted.

"What good is this net? It's a brand new net!"

One of the old deck hands took his pipe out of his mouth and spat over the side, "He's just as right as we are," he muttered.

Captain Kinghorn said the tug returned to St. John Harbour by dark, "and our prayers were answered. We never saw a sign of that submarine."

With true tongue-in-cheek humour Jean Sweet adds:

"Looking back to the day I heard the story it must have been a very yellow submarine – hiding from such a naval force. Perhaps its commander figured nothing could win against the raw courage of the young Canadian Navy.

"If Pink-cheeks survived that war and the others, I hope he can chuckle a little about it now, too. Under orders, he made one of the bravest efforts in Canadian naval history."dd

Saint John's Labour Bells

When the bells of Saint John rang out over the centuries they did more than warn of fire, toll the hour or summon the faithful. Some of them made a political statement of their time.

One, located at the Loyalist landing site at Market Slip, was the cause of considerable controversy between labour and management.

When Local 273 of the International Longshoremen's Association, received its international charter in 1849 (believed to be the first in Canada) its 400 members, known as the Labourers' Benevolent Association, asked for a bell. The purpose of this bell was to mark the hours of Canada's first 10-hour working day and to herald the Saturday "cash" pay day.

But the merchants of North and South wharves at Market Slip (now better known as the Market Square area) were not happy about having a "Labour Bell" placed there and they petitioned the City Council forthwith, demanding the bell be silenced. The reason they gave was that they thought it might disturb the clerks at their work.

City Council complied with their wishes.

But neither the merchants nor the Council had reckoned on the actions of a Freeman of the city named John E. Turnbull, himself a local merchant.

In July of 1849 Turnbull, in defiance of the city's order, leaped on a barrel, addressed the crowd and rang out the first 10-hour work day in Canada. A policeman is said to have noted the incident and looked the other way and the dissenters withdrew, en masse.

Opposition to the Labour Bell gradually faded after that and it rang regularly until November 20,1923, at which time it was presented to the Longshoremen's Union and later to Stella Maris Church in East Saint John, where it still hangs today.

In the meantime, a second Labour Bell was installed at Market Square in West Saint John, across the harbour from Market Slip. This bell, made by the Hooper Company of New Maryland, first tolled on May 23, 1851. It was later used as a fire alarm for many years until a fire alarm system was introduced.

Records indicate that St. Jude's Anglican Church in West Saint John received a bell in January of 1898, after the church was rebuilt following a disastrous fire on February 5,1893. It is believed this was the West Saint John Laborers' Bell which now hangs in St. Jude's Church steeple, from where it has summoned the faithful for nearly a century.

In 1851 a bell tower, which met with mixed reactions to its aesthetic qualities, was erected in the centre of King's Square, located up the King Street hill from Market Slip. The tower was embellished in 1860 for the visit of the Prince of Wales and the tower and the bell therein remained the official fire warning centre until 1877 ... the year of The Great Saint John Fire.

That fire caused devastation to the city, including another of its bells ... Trinity Church bell, which had been installed in 1792, was destroyed along with the church in 1877.

New bells rose from the ashes of that fire. One of

them has brought its history along to its new resting place in King's Square where it hangs today, commemorating the firemen of Saint John who have lost their lives in the line of duty.

This particular bell was struck on order of the City Council and was installed on November 3, 1878. Until 1959 it was housed in a tower above the old Saint John Police Department headquarters on King Street East, just behind the old stone Court House which still commands the best view of King's Square.

From its high tower the bell could be heard for miles around but gradually its usefulness came to an end and its clacker was muffled, save for high days and holidays.

For nearly 30 years its two-ton mass tarnished in the depths of the city's maintenance garage. Now, thanks to the efforts of the Saint John Firemen's Protective Association, Local Union No 771 IAFF and the City of Saint John it hangs in polished splendour in King's Square, commemorating the Saint John Fire Department Bicentennial, 1786-1986.dd

The Little Tower that could ... but never did

Early in the 18th Century and halfway into the 19th Century circular towers on high promontories were all the rage in defence production. In all, sixteen such towers were constructed in British North America, one of those sixteen was placed in Carleton, on the outskirts of what was then called the City of St. John.

They were called "martello" towers a name believed to be derived from Mortella Point, a place on the island of Corsica where a coastal tower manned by a small French force successfully withstood a British naval attack in 1794.

The British were impressed.

So impressed that they built them by the dozens, along their own southeast coast as well as in British North America. And they kept on building them for nearly fifty years and some of them remain to this day, among them the Carleton Martello Tower in Saint John West.

It stands there, majestically towering over a modern panoply of bungalows, container ships and nuclear plants, ready to defend them all after two hundred years of guard duty.

Although it was originally ordered built in Carleton in 1813 to protect the City of St. John from attack during the War of 1812, it wasn't completed until 1815.

During the First World War, from 1914 to 1918, it

**The Carleton Martello Tower secret weapon ...
was it a real cemetery?**

was again alerted for duty, and yet again in the Second
World War from 1939 to 1945, then again during the
Cold War and during any skirmishes that could threaten
Canada from the Bay of Fundy.

And never a shot was fired from it.

And never a shot was fired upon it.

But it was always prepared ... and still is, although
designated now as an historical site and tourist attraction.

The walls and ceilings of the Martello Tower were
designed to withstand fire from both naval guns and land-
based artillery pieces. A parapet nearly two metres high
surrounded the roof providing protection for soldiers

manning the guns who could fire on attackers from a platform called a banquette.

The Carleton Martello Tower had an extra bit of protection from the landward side, that is possibly unique to it. According to David Goss, an historian with deep roots in Carleton, there used to be a small cemetery on the leeward side. The few tombstones scattered through it proved a greater barrier than any mortar, and the soldiers manning the tower didn't fear attack from there. Not because of ghostly protection and such fears the enemy might harbour but because in those days of honour among enemies, soldiers would not desecrate the graves of their opponents.

Of course there's a punch line that has come down through the oral history of the area. There are those who maintain that some clever strategists just planted the tombstones there ... that it wasn't a real cemetery at all!dd

Sweet Violets
Sweeter than all the Roses[1]

As an 'Inner City' kid, growing up in Saint John during the '30s, my knowledge of flowers was sketchy at best. I did know violets to see because they, along with Mayflowers, were sold every spring by Mic Mac Indian women at the Charlotte Street entrance to the City Market.

Of course I was familiar with the Valentine's Day couplet *Roses are red Violets are blue Sugar is sweet And so are you,* but it wasn't until I moved to what was, at that time, the Shiretown of Hampton that violets became more real to me.

Not only did we name our pig "Sweet Violet" ... in tune with the vaudeville rendition of:

Sweet Violets
Sweeter than all the Roses
Covered all over from head to foot
Covered all over with
... ... Sweet Violets ...

... but I was also vaguely aware that it was our provincial flower.

But Oh! What I did not know about that little blossom!

Shrinking violet?
Never!
The violet, my dears, belongs in a select and pres-

tigious company of four which includes the rose, the lily and the chrysanthemum. The only four flowers on earth to achieve political status!

The rose, of course, in England (Irish Roses are romantic, not political!); the chrysanthemum in Japan and the lily in France ... where the Bonaparte family defied tradition and claimed the violet as its emblem.

When Napoleon was banished to Elba the violet became more prominent than ever, the Emperor himself was referred to as "Caporal la Violette" or "Papa la Violette" to symbolize that, like the violet, he would return in the spring.

And, sure enough, in the spring the violets bloomed and, in harmony with their spirit, Napoleon escaped from Elba and returned to France.

The magic of his name opened one city after another to his triumphant advances and his beloved violets were everywhere. The ladies, assembled to meet him as he entered Tuileries on March 20, 1815, wore violet-colored gowns and carried great bunches of the flowers which they showered upon him, while bushels and bushels of violets were thrown beneath his feet.

Although the story of the violet is entwined with the history of France and the Bonaparte family I recently discovered that its remarkable history predates Napoleon by centuries.

The origin of the violet is in Greek mythology which claims that, because of Juno's jealousy, Jupiter turned Io into a heifer then created the violet for her to feed on, since common grass was far too gross to serve the sweetheart of a god.

The Athenians believed that not only was the violet beautiful to behold and fragrant to inhale but that it had magical properties which would ward off drunkenness.

Mohammed, who cultivated and studied flowers, favoured the violet, calling it the "Flower of Humility."

The prophet is quoted as saying, "As my religion is above all others, so is the excellence of the odour of violets above all other odours. It is as warmth in winter and coolness in summer."

In Elizabethan times a book on manners and customs recommends a prescription containing roses, violets, capers, feverfew, saffron, rosemary, sweet apples, scordium, wine, tobacco and cider as a cure for the "dumps" (a dull, gloomy state of mind).

Ancient cookbooks abound with recipes in which the use of the violet is featured ... even to the extent of being 'planted' in one mixture.

The violet has moved poets and prophets to flowery poetry and prose, enchanted the gods, motivated emperors and seduced monarchs with its delicate fragrance, yet it remains a delicate but simple flower.

"These mere bits of prettiness, like a knot of ribbon or a fall of lace upon the costume of a charming girl," according to turn-of-the-century writer N. Hudson Moore are "ornamental but of little use ...... Yet they have defied the scholars who have waged wordy wars over the reasons for its shape, stem, colour and pollen characteristics."

When the woman we today call "The Queen Mom" visited Saint John in 1939, early in the reign of her husband, King George VI, it was known that she was fond of violets. An editorial in the Saint John paper suggested that since "tens of thousands of people are coming into Saint John from the country" for the Royal Visit, they should gather masses of violets.

"The woods are at present full of violets. In water or with damp moss around the stalks they keep fresh for days."

This "huge bouquet for the Queen," the editorial continues, "could be massed near the Royal train."

Whether the "huge bouquet" ever became a reality I don't know but a subsequent article notes that the Renforth Wolf Cubs got a letter from the Queen expressing her thanks for the violets.

The boys had picked the blossoms in the woods back of Renforth and they formed a batch six feet square. These were placed in a large basket and presented to the Queen at the Union Station depot. When the Royal train left Saint John and passed through Renforth, on the way to Moncton, the Cub pack stood at the alert as the Queen waved ... and they were delighted to see their basket of violets displayed in a Royal Train window!

A *Toronto Star* article of May 20, 1941 was datelined "Somewhere in England," and told of a bowl of "wild Canadian violets, a gift from the Queen, which brought a breath of home to the austere, blue-walled mess-room of a central Ontario regiment.

"In the midst of Britain's battle, her majesty remembered the regiment of which she is Colonel-in-Chief with this feminine touch, and through all the Canadian camps in England these are the only really Canadian flowers. They were grown from roots the Queen brought from Canada after the Royal Visit."

The violet, with its multicultural background, is an ideal symbol for bilingual New Brunswick and often is used to label New Brunswick-grown products.

Oh yes! I almost forgot ... nearly everywhere in the world it is believed that to dream of the violet is sure to bring good luck. dd

[1]English Vaudeville song written by Jos. Emmet in 1882, adapted by W.C. Powell in 1908, revised and adapted in 1951 and recorded by Dina Shore.

UFO experiences in New Brunswick

Personal encounters on the road to UFO recognition

It was, I think, about 1956 when I had my closest encounter of any kind with the world of flying saucers.

My husband's company was representing the Jacquays Stark Company of Montreal and we had made friends with the company owner, Morton Jacquays.

I soon discovered that here was a fascinating man with an equally fascinating family and lifestyle.

At the time I was a neophyte in the writing world and Mort thought I might be interested in visiting their farm in the Eastern Townships of Quebec, with the idea of developing a story.

I have never forgotten my experiences there. The Jacquays' estate was unique in the 1950's world of instant chemical solutions. It may well have been the only truly organic farm operating in Canada at that time.

Yes, I got a story. An unbelievable story, as it turned out, because every paper or magazine I sent it to treated it as such. The inference was that the Jacquays were kooks and I was probably a member of the Kook Klub.

The farm was a place where imaginative people with enquiring minds congregated to establish a loose-knit, high-end style commune. These people were concerned about the chemicals in food, the soil and the fertilizer used to feed that soil. They were concerned about the toxins and pollution in medications and about the education of their children in the public schools.

During my week there I met a witch registered with the Parapsychological Research Foundation,London, England; a homeopathic pharmacologist; a UFOlogist, a Montesourri School teacher (one of only a handful of such schools in Canada at the time) and enjoyed a carrot juice cocktail at the farm of the famous Madame Benoit, a neighbour and one of Canada's earliest pioneers in the move toward natural food production.

Forty years later the experiences and conversations I enjoyed during my visit to the Townships remain vivid in my memory. Now, as I begin my research into UFO sightings and experiences in New Brunswick, I wish I could find my notes and the names of the people I met who were dedicated to the belief that our world was being visited by a higher intelligence more sophisticated than the most imaginative science fiction writers of the time ever created.

Around the time I began working on this book a brief news item appeared in *The Telegraph-Journal*: Prof. John Mack, a psychiatrist at Harvard Medical School, was accused of "affirming the delusions" of his patients because he said aliens "have invaded our physical reality" and are affecting the lives of reasonable people.

Despite these accusations, which followed the 1994 publication of the book *Abduction*, written by Prof. Mack, Harvard Medical School affirmed Prof. Mack's full status. Numerous prominent academics came forward to support the author.

Great news for Prof. Mack, for those in New Brunswick and every province and territory in Canada whose sightings of Unidentified Flying Objects (UFOs) have been piquing their curiosity for decades.

To date, I have only been able to find one person in New Brunswick who, at least from what she can remember, may have experienced an abduction.

What New Brunswick does have, in addition to sightings, is Stanton T. Friedman, nuclear physicist, author, researcher and acknowledged expert on UFO sightings and ET

Stanton T. Friedman, New Brunswick world authority on UFO information.

(Extra Terrestrial) occurrences: and people like Christopher Buczynski who has pursued information on UFOs as a hobby for nearly 20 years.

Like Friedman, I have not personally experienced a UFO sighting, nor have I encountered an extra terrestrial being or have I any memories of abductions. Although a neighbour and friend maintains that after returning from her shift as a nursing supervisor that she did, indeed, see a UFO outside my house one night. She went home and described the sighting to her husband who believes with her that it was of an extra terrestrial origin ... I wish they had called me that night!

Nevertheless I did sit in the same room with Hazel Davis and Dr. Peter King as Hazel relived her experiences of 50 and more years ago and those experiences appeared very real to me.

Do I really believe that Earth has been visited by beings and vehicles from worlds beyond those we know?

I do, and I hope I live long enough to recognize some of them.

Anyone of my generation who, over the past 50 or 60 years has watched aircraft equivalent to a motorized box-kite evolve into a vessel that lands people on the moon, takes photographs of Mars and Venus and Saturn's and Jupiter's rings ... must be going through life half-asleep if they can't imagine the reality of space travel!

It's just a matter of time.

I spent a great deal of time reading up on what has been said and done about UFOs and ETs over the years,(some of them, including the hoaxes, chronicled in newspaper headlines as early as the mid -19th Century) before presenting this book for publication .

Much of my research was done through *The Encyclopedia of UFOs* edited by Ronald D. Story and published in 1979. Story is a dedicated UFOlogist and an honest researcher. His encyclopedia includes the pros and the cons of the existence of UFOs.

I was intrigued to read psychiatrist Carl Jung's concept of UFOs, ETs, ghosts and poltergeist ... all of which he lumps together as examples of "the new mythology."

UFOs are, he says, "the Gods of the Age of Science." He did not deny their possible reality.

Canadian researcher and writer Arthur Reid Bray, a retired pilot in the Royal Canadian Air Force and more recently retired from his position as head of the Canada Safety Council, told me his position on UFOs etc. has not changed from that he espoused when he wrote the book *The Science, The Public & The UFO* in 1967. He has always believed the parallel universe theory ...

"... some may be members of our ancestral race ... studies indicate that life in many forms exists throughout the universe and that there are parallel universes superimposed on the physical universe we know. A major flaw in our thinking is to expect that an alien intelligence would necessarily behave as we would."

Two pieces of metal, found on the shore of the St. Lawrence River at Les Écureuils, were written about by

Bray back in 1960. He described one of them as follows: *the largest piece was 70 1/2 inches by 54 inches, 24 inches at the centre, shaped like an oblong inverted mushroom and weighing about 3,000 lbs. It showed evidence of melting and crushing and at the top centre there were the remains of two pipes, one about six inches in diameter with a two inch bore; the other, two inches in diameter with a 1 1/2 inch bore.*

Numerous reports were done on the metal but no two laboratory results agreed in their findings of what metal(s) it was, let alone what object it was.

Speaking from his home in Ottawa, Bray said, "I'm still open-minded about it." The last he heard someone in Toronto was working on the metal, still trying to un- earth its secret.

While much so-called evidence of UFOs has been pooh-poohed by scientists and governments a great deal still remains unexplained. Even the comprehensive study commissioned in 1966 by the Secretary of the U.S. Air Force and headed by Dr. Edward U. Condon, physicist and theoretician in the Department of Physics and Astrophysics at the University of Colorado, was unable to explain 40 per cent of the cases, despite Dr. Condon's stated disbelief in their credibility.

Among those the Commission was unable to dis- prove were a sighting in Alberta, which included both visual testimony and photographs, and the BOAC stratocruiser sighting while flying over Labrador.

"This unusual sighting should therefore be as- signed to the category of some almost certainly natural phenomenon which is so rare that it apparently has never been reported before or since."

In the August 21, 1965 issue of the *Christian Science Monitor* the science editor wrote: *Flying saucers are all but literally knocking on the laboratory door ... some-*

thing definitely is going on that cannot yet be explained.

When did such sightings begin? One of the earliest chronicles of what appears to be a classic "Flying Saucer" can be found in the first chapter of the Prophet Ezekiel in the Old Testament. I've taken the liberty of copying most of it here to lead off this section on UFOs.

There are so many things from the early history of man that cannot be explained through simple history that I, for one, believe we are part of something far greater than we have been able to comprehend. It is the basis of what we call religion. The big questions, of course, are: *How many layers of life are there? Is life infinite?*

Philosophy is for another time, for now let's just look at what we know of in recent history.

UFO sightings peaked in 1966 and 1967, waned then peaked again 10 years later, in 1977-78 and they have continued sporadically for over a century. They continue today, with less attention from the media.

Perhaps we have become blasé and we are no longer surprised. Perhaps *Star Trek* has done its job too well! dd

What the Prophet Ezekiel saw

[1]*Ezek'l saw de wheel, Ezek'l saw de wheel*
    'Way up in de middle of de air.
    De big wheel move by faith;
De little wheel move by de grace of God;
    A wheel in a wheel,
    Way up in de middle of de air.
A wheel in a wheel, a wheel in a wheel,
    Ezek'l saw de wheel,
'Way up in de middle of de air.

How many Biblical chronicles contain references that might lend themselves to descriptions of Unidentified Flying Objects?

I don't know if anyone has ever tried to count them but certainly there has been great speculation over the visions of God or her angels and what they might mean. Excerpts of the most specific of these was read by Harvey McLeod on CBC's Saint John Main Street program, from the Book of the Prophet Ezekiel in the Old Testament. Some of the text follows but for those who would like to read the entire Book of Ezekiel I suggest starting at Chapter 1 and decide what you think Ezekiel saw ... and hum a few bars of the [1] Black American Spiritual as recorded (1926), popularized as *Ezekiel Saw a Wheel a-Rollin' Way in the Middle of the Air!*

The first two verses establish the time and the year as being the thirtieth year in the fourth month on the fifth day of the month. As a point of reference Ezekiel identifies it as being the fifth year of King Jehoiachin's captivity.

A delightful conversation with Rabbi Spiro of Fredericton further set the time frame for me as 593BC, or more graphically 2,589 years ago. He also added that the "towers" referred to in the Book of Isaiah,Ch.33, are called "flying towers" in the Talmud. Rabbie Spiro's inference being that perhaps these, too, represented some kind of UFO.

What Ezekiel Saw

... And I looked, and, behold, a whirlwind came out of the north, a great cloud, and a fire infolding itself, and a brightness was about it , and out of the midst thereof as the colour of amber, out of the midst of the fire.

Also out of the midst thereof came the likeness of four living creatures. And this was their appearance; they had the likeness of a man.

And every one had four faces and every one had four wings.

And their feet were straight feet; and the sole of their feet was like the sole of a calf's foot; and they sparkled like the colour of burnished brass.

And they had the hands of a man under their wings on their four sides; and the four had their faces and their wings.

Their wings were joined one to another; they turned not when they went; they went every one straight forward.

As for the likeness of their faces, they four had the face of a man, and the face of a lion, on the right side; and they four had the face of an ox on the left side; they four also had the face of an eagle.

A wheel in a wheel,
    Way up in de middle of de air.
A wheel in a wheel, a wheel in a wheel,
    Ezek'l saw de wheel,
  'Way up in de middle of de air.

Thus were their faces; and their wings were stretched upward; two wings of every one were joined one to another and two covered their bodies.

And they went every one straight forward; whither the spirit was to go, they went; and they turned not when they went.

As for the likeness of the living creatures, their appearance was like burning coals of fire, and like the appearance of lamps; it went up and down among the living creatures; and the fire was bright and out of the fire went forth lightning.

And the living creatures ran and returned as the appearance of a flash of lightning.

Now as I beheld the appearance of the living creatures, behold one wheel upon the earth by the living creatures, with his four faces.

The appearance of the wheels and their work was like unto the colour of a beryl; and they four had one likeness; and their appearance and their work was as it were a wheel in the middle of a wheel.

When they went, they went upon their four sides; and they turned not when they went.

As for their rings, they were so high that they were dreadful; and their rings were full of eyes round about them four.

And when the living creatures went, the wheels went by them; and when the living creatures were lifted up from the earth the wheels were lifted up.

Whithersoever the spirit was to go, they went, thither was their spirit to go; and the wheels were lifted up over against them; for the spirit of the living creature was in the wheels.

When those went, these went and when those stood, these stood and when those were lifted up from the earth, the wheels were lifted up over against them; for the spirit of the living creature was in the wheels.

And the likeness of the firmament upon the heads of the living creature was as the colour of the terrible crystal, stretched forth over their heads above.

And under the firmament were their wings straight, the one toward the other; every one had two, which covered on this side, and everyone had two, which covered on that side, their bodies.

And when they went, I heard the noise of their wings, like the noise of great waters, as the voice of the Almighty, the voice of speech, as the noise of an host; when they stood, they let down their wings.

And there was a voice from the firmament that was over their heads, when they stood, and had let down their wings.

And above the firmament that was over their heads was the likeness of a throne, as the appearance of a sapphire stone: and upon the likeness of the throne was the likeness as the appearance of a man above upon it.

And I saw as the colour of amber, as the appearance of fire round about within it, from the appearance of his loins even upward, and from the appearance of his loins even downward, I saw as it were the appearance of fire, and it had brightness round about.

As the appearance of the bow that is in the cloud in the day of rain, so was the appearance of the brightness round about. This was the appearance of the likeness of the glory of the Lord. And when I saw it, I fell upon my face, and I heard a voice of one that spake.

And so endeth Chapter 1.

Fascinating stuff! dd

Chronology of UFO Sightings in New Brunswick

1936 or 1937
early July-   Barnesville area in St. John/Kings counties

1945 or 1946
Winter-   Barnesville area, St. John County

1965
July 18 -   Fredericton centre
July ????   Lint Farm, Royal Road, Fredericton

1970 or 71-
Late to
mid-June-   Western sky in City of Saint John

1973
Nov. 22-   Chatham, at Glenwood, Northumberland
              County,NB

1977
May 14 -   Titusville, Kings County

1978
Feb. 9-   Base Gagetown @ 3 a.m. Ball of fire travelling
              from West to East
March 26-   As many as 28 Miramichiers report seeing
              something unusual in the sky.
              Reports from: Oyster River near Neguac,
              Bartibobog Bridge, from car travelling on
              Highway 11; All in Northumberland
              County.
June 7.   Bathurst, 1/2 mile from bridge near pulp
              mill

1979
May 29,   Rogersville area, Northumberland County.
May 30.   near Notre-Dame on Highway 11,
               Northumberland County.

1980
Feb. 12,   Lower Newcastle

1988
Aug. 22
or early
Aug. 23   Near Hanwell Road in Fredericton

1990
Jan. 20
or there-
abouts,   St. Pons near Tracadie
1992
Jan. 22   Ten sightings at various locations between
               Victoria Corner and Florenceville in
               Victoria and Carleton Counties.
1993
Nov. 1.   Chatham Head, Northumberland County
Nov. 4.   Baie Ste. Anne, Northumberland County
Nov.30.   Douglastown, Northumberland County
Dec. 15.   Perth Andover, Victoria County

1995
Summer-   Moncton from Shediac Road

1996
March 3   Near Mazerolle Settlement Fredericton area

Fredericton's Royal Road sight of UFO landing in the 1960s

As I thumbed through the folder titled "UFOs," as collected by Eliza Aitken in Fredericton's *Daily Gleaner* Library, I came across a slip of paper simply saying "call Doreen Hazlett, Royal Road."

So I called Doreen Hazlett who put me on to her husband, Bev. Hazlett. Thus began my search for information on the reported landing of a UFO on the farm of one Walter Lint, McLeod's Hill, Royal Road.

Mr. Lint was reluctant to talk to me about the event, saying he didn't want to again put up with what he went through at that time. He implied that people had made him feel foolish and he wanted no more to do with the affair.

I understood his concern and I was sympathetic but I was also eager to learn more of the "landing" of a UFO in New Brunswick. Everyone I talked to about the sighting was sure that it happened anywhere from 1967 to 1972 and I diligently combed the *Fredericton Gleaner and Telegraph Journal* files in those years seeking some reference to it.

I found nothing!

I decided to go public with my quest and called Kevin Ryan, CBC Fredericton's Main Street host. Thanks to Kevin and CBC who aired my dilemma I got the Royal Road story and reports of three more sightings over the years in the Fredericton area.

In 1965, Dr. David Wade, now a Fredericton dentist, was a university student working at a summer construction job. On July 18 of that year he, and his twin brother, dropped off David's girlfriend at her home at the top of Regent Street and were about to return to their own Main Street home when they looked up and saw a strange "Robin's egg blue light overhead."

Here are David's stories:

"I kept looking out the car window and the light seemed to be following us all the way down the hill. When we got home we got my mother, Dorothy Wade, and my grandmother, Lily DeLong, to come out and look at it too. By this time we could hear it making a humming sound and we could see a little red light and a big arch effect then, quite suddenly, it headed downriver toward the airport.

"My mother went in and called the airport and they said a lot of people had been calling them but they knew of no aeroplane or helicopter to be in the air around Fredericton at that time.

"When my mother came back out and told us this we were still watching in the direction it had gone, then suddenly it came back again.

"I can remember we weren't at all afraid of it, just excited and my brother and I were so excited we were jumping up and down, we were hoping to get a look inside, or talk to them or something."

Whatever it was went away again and didn't come back. The next day after work David went to the library and got out every book or bit of information on UFOs that he could find. Since then he and his brother continue to be interested in UFOs and keen observers.

"It was just a short time after that we heard about the sighting at the Lint farm, over on the Royal Road. My

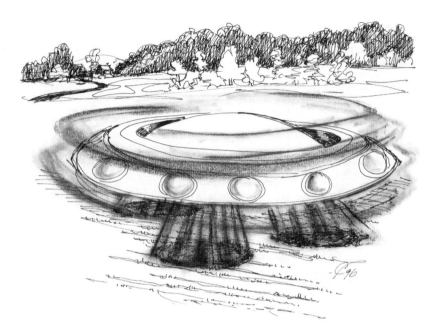

" *The girls told us they had seen it a couple of nights before and described it as having glowing plates, the size of dinner plates, all the way around it.*"

brother and I and another friend went over to the farm.

"I think it was one of Mr. Lint's daughters who took us out to the field ... they were just as excited about it as we were ...

"It was just after the hay had been cut and they showed us three circular indentations in the grass. The three indentations marked out a circular area of about 30 feet. The girls told us they had seen it a couple of nights before and described it as having glowing plates, the size of dinner plates, all the way around it."

There had been a number of sightings around that time, he said, then they seemed to stop for a while.

"A few years ago, and I don't remember just when it was my brother, who is also a dentist, told me about a patient of his who was driving out the Killarney Road and as she went around a series of turns she suddenly spotted a long, cigar-shaped object through her back window. She pulled over to the side of the road and stopped. She said it was as big as a football field and several cars, including an RCMP car, also stopped along the road to watch it until it disappeared."

Then, in the evening of July 20, 1989, David's wife was outside looking up at the Aurora Borealis when what looked like a huge boomerang suddenly appeared in the sky.

"About 20 of us gathered around to look at it. It was really strange because it wasn't in the lights of the Aurora but in the black sky and, although it was brown against the black sky it was very plain and easy to see ... yet there was no vapour, no lights and it just disappeared after awhile."

David Wade says in each of the above noted instances he advised Dr. Stanton Friedman of the sightings but never reported them to any official organization. dd

'It hung there long enough for me to get a good look at it'

Telegraph-Journal columnist Robert Neilsen's reflections should leave no doubt in readers' minds that he is a down-to-earth-no-nonsense pragmatist if ever there was one. To think of Neilsen as being a fanciful man would appear to be as far removed from his nature as it would be to expect him to endorse the philosophy of same-sex marriages.

For this reason it is doubly interesting to read his account of a UFO sighting he, his wife Betty and other people in the Perth-Andover area, experienced.

On Dec. 15, 1993 they saw what appeared to be a light, with smaller lights underneath it, about 100 to 150 feet above the St. John River in clear view of their home.

"It hung there for some time," Neilsen said. "The light underneath revolved and was more red than the one above, which was more the colour of an ordinary light bulb.

"It hung there long enough for me to go outside and get a better look at it, then it very slowly began to move up-river. It was a cloudy night ... "

When I asked if he could give me a size comparison, Neilsen thought for a few minutes then said, "people used to say the moon was as big as a dinner plate and if you use that as a comparison then what I saw would have been about the size of an old-fashioned wash-tub.

"The larger light above was a few feet above the bottom, it was perhaps as much as 70 ft. wide. We couldn't see anything in the form of a connection between the two lights. It was silent, There was no noise.

"Quite a few other people saw it.

"It struck me as odd that any alien creatures ... if there are such things ... Why would they want to be investigating us?"

At the time of the sighting Loring Air Base in Maine was about 30 miles north of where the Neilsens live, a fact that may be a contributing factor to the sighting. The base is now closed but Neilsen believes the closure of the Loring Air Base had been announced by then but it had not yet closed.

"It's the only thing up here that might have any attraction for visitors from space. Recently I read the following witticism that I found quite pithy: *The surest sign of intelligent life in outer space is that they have not yet tried to contact us.*"

Mr. Neilsen is not without experiences in the fourth dimension. Among them are déja vu occurrences, precognition and ESP. The most dramatic, however, was being faced with a geometry problem he had never seen or heard of before and being able to present a correct solution to it in a matter of seconds.

"All I can say is that it was a very strange feeling. I am by no means a math scholar." dd

1992 ... A big year
for Carleton County sightings

There had been one earlier sighting in the area covered by the *Hartland Observer*, Wendy Marr said.

"I don't know just when it was and it doesn't seem to have been very well documented ... but 1992 is another story. We even have a video and at least ten people who sighted the first one, on Jan.22. Then, on April 6, eleven residents reported similar sightings. There haven't been any since, despite the fact that people were really watching the skies by then."

In Wendy's story in the *Hartland Observer* of Feb. 5 she reported that several area residents thought they were part of a science fiction movie ... or an episode of *Unsolved Mysteries* ... when they glanced skyward and saw an aircraft unlike any they had ever seen before.

The sightings were in various locations between the areas of Victoria Corner and Florenceville and they took place between the hours of seven and eight-thirty in the evening.

Three adults in the Rosedale-Victoria Corner area, who wished to remain anonymous, spoke to world-recognized Unidentified Flying Object specialist and nuclear physicist Stanton Friedman. He summed up their description of the object as being triangular with unblinking red and orange lights on the bottom and a triangular pattern of lights behind it.

Described as having "a quiet jet noise" the object moved in a steady pattern ... back and forth ... low to the horizon yet fairly close.

One witness did say he/she had observed a similar aircraft in the area a month earlier.

A nine-minute video tape taken by one of these witnesses was sent to the United States for viewing by UFO expert Dr. Bruce Macabee who, Mr. Friedman said, confirmed that it was not in any way doctored or tampered with. While the object on the tape remains unidentified the failure, in the taping process, to include reference points which could be used as scales for measuring it made it impossible to judge size and distance.

Numerous other observers came forward independently and all offered confirming testimony to its shape and lighting characteristics.

One observer, who watched for three or four minutes, thought at first it was an aeroplane but because it wasn't moving he thought it was a helicopter. He was driving straight toward it and drove underneath. At that time he saw five white lights in a circle on one end and two or three red lights off to the right side. He described the lights as very bright and quite stationary.

Yet another observer described a similar object which he watched for about twenty minutes while travelling from Hartland to Florenceville. As he travelled toward his home in Florenceville the aircraft changed direction twice and, for a period of time, he was able to estimate its speed.

He said he was going at about 80km/h and believes the object was travelling at around 90km/h to 94km/h. He described it as bigger than a plane that would normally fly at that speed. An experienced pilot, he said an aircraft of the size he saw would normally travel at a minimum airspeed of 180km- 200km/h.

His initial reaction was that it was an aircraft in distress and he wondered why there were no lights on at the nearby McCain's airfield. He also said he thought it had a lot more lights on it than an ordinary aeroplane would have.

When he followed it from behind the lights were very bright then, when it turned sideways, the lights were flashing.

Although this particular observer thought the behaviour of the aircraft was not what he would normally expect from an aeroplane he steadfastly maintains that he does not believe that alien spacecraft exist.

When Carla Orser noticed a cluster of yellow and white lights in the sky over the Somerville area, while working upstairs in her home, she stopped and watched them. They were visible between seven-thirty and seven forty-five in the evening before they suddenly disappeared.

From his home on the St. Thomas Road Richard Orser also noticed something strange in the sky. After seeing white lights outside his living room window he went to his front door to get a closer look.

"As soon as I opened the door a red flame shot out the back and it took off. It was going really fast," he said.

Then, ten to fifteen minutes later while he was still outside, a second aircraft flew directly over the house about 200 feet in the air. He heard what he described as "a jet noise" and noted that there were four or five lights on the bottom of the aircraft.

On April 6 when Clayton Shaw looked out his bedroom window at around ten-thirty in the evening he saw a bright light which he estimated to be 200 ft. in the air. He called the rest of his family to come out on the deck and they watched the object for about two minutes before it turned and went away only to return and go again three times at four minute intervals. They had watched a similar sight in January at around six o'clock while they were eating supper.

Murray and Toby Underhill from Bennett's Lake Road in Rosedale also saw the strange lights for the second time. They had video-taped their first sighting over a two hour period for a total of nine minutes of taped sighting. On April 6 they were called by the Shaws to come to Rosedale to tape what they were seeing. The April sighting was not so vivid as that in January and the tapes did not come out as well.

At about one-thirty a.m. they saw a large, bright light moving fast across the sky before disappearing.

The above material was gleaned from the pages of the Hartland Observer *and through conversations with Wendy Marr and Stanton Friedman. dd*

Mysterious black triangle seen hovering Over Moncton

Julien Daigle of Moncton has been interested in UFOs for a number of years and hopes someday to do research in the field. He recently joined a select group from New Brunswick who belong to MUFON (the Mutual Unidentified Flying Object Network) and subsequently wrote to nuclear physicist Stanton T. Friedman to share the following experience:

In the Fall of 1995 Julien made an oral presentation on UFOs and extraterrestrial evidence to his grade 11 English class at Mathieu Martin High School, "never in a million years expecting that a classmate would be among the privileged few to have experienced a sighting.

"Following my presentation one of my classmates explained to me that she had a sighting in that summer (1995). The sighting was made with her mother at sunset while they were driving along the Shediac Road in Moncton. It consisted of a triangular-shaped UFO," he wrote Friedman.

The student, 16 year-old Julie Robichaud, shared the following story and sketch for publication here.

"At first I thought I was seeing some sort of weird aircraft. I've always been fascinated with aeroplanes and, as I watched it, I was thinking how big it was and wondering what it was doing down so low. 'What if it's a UFO?' I asked myself and then I said, 'No. It couldn't be!'

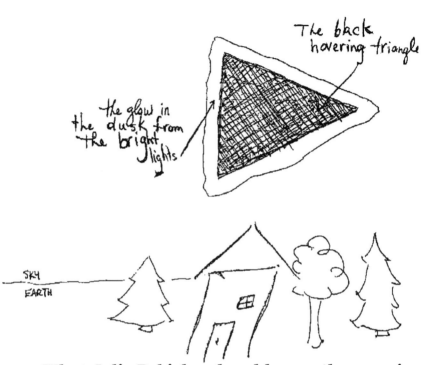

Julie's sketch of the UFO

The black hovering triangle

the glow in the dusk from the bright lights

SKY
EARTH

What Julie Robichaud and her mother saw in Moncton in the Fall of 1995.

But then I didn't really see what else it could be. Of course my mother still thinks it was some kind of an aeroplane. She doesn't believe in UFOs."

What Julie and her mother saw was a "huge triangular-shaped object that hovered over a house in a subdivision beside the road. It would have been to the East because the sunset was behind us.

"It was a solid black triangle and there were no lights at the edges, like there would be on an aircraft's wings, but it was as if there was a light above it that illuminated it around the edges, shimmering like heat on a hot summer day. Even though it was August, it was not a hot day.

"As we watched, it suddenly swerved sideways then took off and just disappeared."

When she got home and told her brother, Denis, about what she saw he told her right away that he believed it was a UFO.

"He reminded me of the time a couple years ago, he was around eleven or twelve years-old at the time, when we were coming home from watching a meteor shower at night. He said at the time that he saw a triangular light in the sky hovering over the University of Moncton. We all thought it was just fantasy on his part but now I'm not so sure, he said what he saw was just like I described.

"It could be true! It could be that we both saw a UFO! Was it the same one both times? Or two different UFOs?" **dd**

Northumberland County sightings span two decades

Why Northumberland County? What earthly ... or perhaps not so earthly ... reason could there be for so many Unidentified Flying Objects to not only be seen in this sprawling, lumbered and lumbering part of the province, but to be so thoroughly chronicled in Canada's Public Archives in Ottawa?

The answer might be the solution, depending on who you talk to on the subject of UFOs. The believer will be convinced the UFOs were there over the years because of CFB Chatham. The nonbeliever will agree, convinced that UFO sightings in the area are nothing more than freak reflections of Chatham aircraft constantly combing the skies for ... What else? ... UFOs.

It's Catch 22 and déja vu all over again!

Thanks to solid coverage in the *Miramichi Leader* by Joanne Cadogan and some official reports, made available by the National Archives, we have a fairly good picture of UFO activity in Northumberland County beginning in 1973.

The earliest, on Nov. 22, 1973, was a sighting by a 13-year-old Glenwood boy who saw a set of lights, two red and two green and one white light, that looked like a revolving search light. The official report, prepared by Cst. D.B. Griffiths of the Newcastle Detachment of the RCMP is quoted here (just as written including the 'X's):

" Cpl. XXX* of the Canadian Forces Base Chatham, NB "called and stated that he had received a phone call from an ex-serviceman who told him that his son had seen an U.F.O. near their residence at the captionally noted location.(Glenwood)

"XXX stated that the caller did not wish to have his name divulged, however, gave his phone number as XXXXX. I asked the caller if there had been any aircraft in the air prior to his call and XXX stated that there had been a helicopter, however, it had landed sometime before receiving the phone call. Checks were made with the Moncton Airport and their radar failed to detect any aircraft in the scope of their radar at the time of the presumed sighting which was approximately 7:15-7:20 p.m.

"I called telephone number XXXX and explained to the gentleman that we would need some information for record purposes. He stated his name was XXXXX and that we could visit his residence and interview his son who had seen the UFO. At 9:30 p.m. I met with XXXXXXX 13 years of age who stated that he had seen a set of lights, two red and two green and one white light which was revolving and looked like a search light. XXXXXXX stated that he had observed this object for approximately two minutes after which time it went out of sight in the vicinity of the abandoned Glenwood School. Further to this, he stated there was no noise being emitted from the object and that it was flying at an altitude of approximately twice the height of trees. XXXXXXX was unable to give any information pertaining to this object's shape and colour. Atmospheric condition in the vicinity of the sighting was misty with a light mist falling.

"XXXXXXX stated that the route which the U.F.O. seemed to be taking was that of a Northeasterly course going from behind his residence on the west side of Highway 11 diagonally across to behind the Glenwood School.

"On 23 Nov 73, I visited the area behind Glenwood School . Mr. Marton Dickson, owner of the School and who resides in a mobile trailer behind the School, stated that he had heard two extremely loud thumps sometime between 7 p.m. - 7:30 p.m. 22 Nov. 73.

"Dickson paid no particular attention to these things as he thought they were caused by a truck going over a bump on Highway 11 a few feet from his home. After telling Dickson my reason for being at his residence and describing to him the supposed course of the U.F.O. he seemed to be more sure that the sound had come from the North side of his trailer which he felt was unusual as two bumps in the road were directly in front of his residence and not North of his residence on Highway 11. Dickson and I searched the area where the U.F.O. seemed to disappear from XXXXXX's view without finding any trace of any foreign object or aircraft having crashed or landed. This area behind the residence is wooded with evergreen trees which seem to be approximately 30-40 ft. in height and behind these trees is a large open swampy area.

"XXXXXXX at the time of his interview was very excited and scared of the consequences of seeing this object, however, I am confident that he did see an object of unknown origin or possibly a helicopter from CFB Chatham, NB doing radar approaches and possibly counter blade rotations.

"I contacted Cpl. XXXX and we both feel that what the observer saw was, indeed, a helicopter approaching the Base, however this cannot be conclusive as the records at CFB Chatham, NB show that the helicopters landed prior to the sighting.

"This report is being submitted as per O.M. CO-

NRC, Para. 7 and a copy of same will be forwarded direct to:

> The Upper Atmospheric Research Section
> Astrophysics Branch
> National Research Council
> Ottawa, Ontario
> K1A OE6

Concluded here

> D.B. Griffiths 26560 Cst.
> Newcastle Det.

(W.H. **Baskin) Sgt.
I/C Newcastle Det."

The names of those involved were blacked out on the report. dd
**This name may not be accurate as photocopy is of poor quality.* dd

It was not until <u>March 26, 1978</u> that another sighting was reported. At that time 28 people from the Miramichi reported seeing something unusual in the sky.

Four people reported seeing two huge, bright fiery reddish-orange objects streak across the sky and apparently crash not far from Bartibog Bridge.

RCMP reports quote one witness as saying the object she saw was about the size of an aeroplane cockpit, was on fire and had a tail on it. The object was seen for about a minute before it fell not too far away in the woods near a field.

The official RCMP report states that Mrs. Mary Dance of RR 2 Douglastown, NB and her son were travelling east on Highway 11 around the Bartibog Bridge area when they noticed two balls of fire in the sky. When they saw the first one they got out of the car to see better. On the way back to the car, they saw another object the same as the first one ... but moving from north to south, towards the Miramichi River. It appeared to be two to three feet in diameter and travelling silently for about two minutes before it simply disappeared.

At the same time Mr. and Mrs. Bernard Savage of Russellville Road noticed a similar incident.

The calls were made to the RCMP around 8 p.m.

The RCMP officer went to the area and, looking from the road, failed to see any tracks that would indicate such an object had crashed or landed there. The officer continued to Base Chatham and contacted Lieut. Austin and made arrangements to make a helicopter trip over the area the following morning.

However, there was no report from the Air Force Base by April 3 and the RCMP constable took it on himself to do some more investigating. He found others who had seen the same sight but who did not report it because they were afraid they would be laughed at.

The constable then contacted a forestry department employee and the two went on skidoos to the area where the witnesses all agreed the impact had occurred. After five hours of patrolling the men could find nothing that would indicate such an occurrence.

In the course of discussion with people of the area the constable discovered at least 15 people had seen the same object but on different dates.

Then, on April 10, Mrs. Walter Cormier of Beresford and three other persons at the same location saw a high green, yellow and red flare moving slowly across the sky. Mrs. Cormier watched it through a telescope for approximately 15 minutes.

In all of the above sightings it was confirmed there were no high level flights over the Chatham terminal control area at the time of the sightings.

On June 7 Charles Best of Bathurst was at his home, half-a-mile from the bridge near the pulp mill,

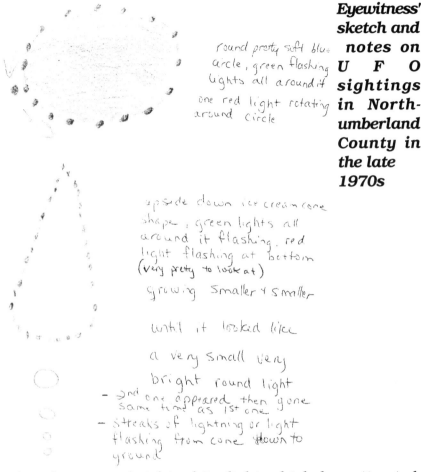

Eyewitness' sketch and notes on U F O sightings in North- umberland County in the late 1970s

round pretty soft blue circle, green flashing lights all around it

one red light rotating around circle

upside down ice cream cone shape, green lights all around it flashing. red light flashing at bottom (very pretty to look at)

growing smaller + smaller

until it looked like

a very small very

bright round light
- 2nd one appeared then gone same time as 1st one
- streaks of lightning or light flashing from cone down to ground

when he saw a bright white light which he estimated was anywhere from 20 to 40 miles north of him. He told the RCMP that it stayed for over an hour before moving across the horizon 15 to 20 degrees to the east.

In 1979 National Research Council of Canada documents again detail a UFO sighting, this time by a Rogersville area man who reported seeing two bright, stationary lights about half-a-mile apart, hovering about 1,000 ft. above the tree line around two miles away. He watched the lights for five minutes before they went down into the trees.

The next day a delivery truck driver was dropping off a newspaper at the CFB Chatham guardhouse and told the MP on duty that he saw a bright orange light "the size of a street light" in the sky over Highway 11 between St. Margarets and Moncton.

Then, on Feb. 12, 1980 a Lower Newcastle couple reported a bright light hovering in the air approximately six miles or more south of Lower Newcastle.

The light appeared to be about 25 or more feet in length and heading in an easterly direction. The couple described the object as being very bright with no markings or lights that might come from a normal aircraft. It was visible for five minutes before moving straight up into cloud cover.

In all these reports the investigating officers said the people they talked to were coherent, rational and sober persons.

It wasn't until 1993 that the sightings began again.

On Nov. 2 that year two separate Chatham Head couples reported seeing a similar red and white flashing object in the night sky shortly after midnight. The incident was written up in *The Miramichi Leader* then promptly pooh-poohed by a man from Maine, who claimed that what they saw was a weather balloon used by ham radio operators to carry their signals.

But the man from Maine was proved wrong when a member of the Radio Amateur Peninsule Club in Tracadie said a team from that group had found the helium-filled balloon, which had been launched from Ottawa on Oct. 30 and contained a special transmitter for use by radio operators. The balloon had splashed down in a swamp early the previous Sunday morning, before the reported sighting. It would have been impossible to spot the balloon anyway, the radio club spokesman said, because it did not contain any bright red and white or indicator lights.

Then, on Nov. 4 Albert Manuel and a friend were out driving when, at about seven-thirty in the evening, they spotted an orange/red light, the size of a basketball, in Baie Ste. Anne.

Manuel said if it was moving it wasn't moving very fast. They didn't get out of the car but they did have the window down and could not hear a sound. When Manuel returned to Baie Ste. Anne he discovered another group of drivers had spotted the strange light from their location, about six miles away.

It was November 30 when the third sighting in the month was reported by a Douglastown couple. The woman first noticed the object when she looked out her kitchen window at around 10 p.m. She said it looked like flashing red and green lights so she went to get binoculars and they went out on the balcony to get a better look. Through the binoculars she saw what looked like a big, round blue circle with a red light that came around every few seconds.

They watched it for an hour until, at 11:10 p.m. it changed shape, looking more like an upside-down ice-cream cone, then within five minutes it began to get smaller and move away. By 11:20 p.m. it was "just a tiny little light" and at 11:25 it was gone. *dd*

Hazel Davis has puzzled over these memories for 60 years

Hazel Davis was only nine years old when she had the first of two experiences with what she now believes was an extraterrestrial presence. That was sixty years ago. It was not until many years later, when Hazel was a married woman raising a family, that the pieces of what were to become fascinating puzzles began to gradually fit into place.

The puzzles are far from complete, despite the competent help of psychologist Dr. Peter King of St. Andrews who hypnotized her and regressed her memory to the time of the events. It was an experiment she had been wanting to carry out and decided to go ahead with at this time.

I had the privilege of being present during this experiment and, because I have been successfully hypnotized on a number of occasions, I feel competent to testify that Hazel Davis appeared to me to be in a deep state of hypnosis. Her experience under hypnosis, and my recorded notes of the event, will be chronicled in the course of her stories.

First it is important to describe the person who is Hazel Davis. At sixty-nine she is both physically and mentally active and alert. When we visited the sites she had described to me, where her experiences took place, she virtually danced over the rough furrows left by yesteryear's plows, eyes sparkling with vivid memories as she compared those sites today with their appearance so many years ago.

Small and soft spoken, Hazel is highly intelligent and well read. She continues to work on a regular basis as a supermarket cashier. In fact just after we began talking I picked up a magazine produced by the supermarket chain she works for and discovered Hazel in full colour, reigning over one-third of a valuable advertising page. She had been honoured by her employer as winner of the "Quarterly Employee Touch Award."

Born Hazel Rogers, she grew up on a 300 acre farm near the Barnesville area, not far from the Hammond River and the Loch Lomond area of Saint John. Today, she makes her home in Saint John but still has close ties with family and friends throughout the rural community she knew so well as a child.

Unfortunately when Dr. King regressed Hazel to her earlier memory there was some confusion in leading her into the event. This was followed by great agitation on Hazel's part followed by a complete blocking of the event.

Her second experience, at the age of 17, came through clearly under hypnosis and there was some minor clarification of the events as she experienced them.

Hazel's first story, *The Dancing Sunbeams*, took place on the family farm.

Her second story, *And Then There Was Light*, took place at her brother's home in an isolated area near Barnesville.

The Dancing Sunbeams

It was a beautiful, hot summer day and I was in the farm house kitchen, having just finished lunch. I'm not sure of an exact date but I remember school was out and, considering what I remember my father saying later, it was before the first cut of hay. That would make it late June or early in July.

And that's what makes my thoughts that day so strange for I sat up suddenly and told my mother and father that I had to go see the flowers, beyond on the hill, before they were all gone.

With that I walked out the kitchen door, crossed the yard and followed the path past the barn and over the hill. I walked down the other side, looking at the flowers nestling their gold and purple heads among the weeds and grass. Then, out of nowhere, a small ball of light about the size of a ping pong ball began dancing among them. I had the fleeting thought that a sunbeam doesn't look like that!

I may have said it aloud, I don't know. I don't know either whether the voice I heard saying, 'Mmmmm,' was a real voice or a voice I heard in my head. I do know it was deep like a man's voice.

Then I heard another noise, a 'Sw-i-i-i-sh-sh, sw-i-i-sh-sh' and I started walking home to the farm.

When I went into the kitchen my mother said,

'Where have you been all afternoon, Hazel? I've been calling you! It's suppertime, Now run and clean up like a good girl.'

Somewhere I had lost a whole afternoon. Where did it go? I can't remember. I do remember feeling as if I was being examined by someone or something ... but I didn't remember any of this until just a few years ago.

It was when I was reading Betty Luca's book <u>The Watchers (The Secret Design Behind UFO Abduction</u> by Raymond E. Fowler, published by Bantam, 1990) and she described the small ball of light she saw when, quite suddenly, the memory of that entire day ... save for those missing afternoon hours ... flashed into my mind.

I remembered wanting to see the flowers, I remembered the dancing light and I remembered the voice ... and I also remember a voice in my head telling me the memories would return when it was the right time.

I slowly began to remember different things, like the incident a few weeks after that when my father was sitting in the kitchen talking to his friend. He was telling him about going up to cut the hay in the field and finding the grass and flowers all twisted and lying flat on the ground in patches; and that he couldn't understand what had happened to them but something had crushed them and the spots were turning brown.

I remember having a guilty feeling at the time, listening to him describe what happened and realizing that I had been anxious to go see the flowers behind the barn ... before they were gone! As if I knew something was going to happen to them.

My father was dead by the time these memories started coming back but my mother was there, too, that day. I asked her if she remembered my father saying about the grass and the flowers but she didn't. I suppose it was too much to expect.

And Then There Was Light

When I was 17 years old I stayed winters with my brother. Although he lived in an isolated area there was a better road which made it easier to get into Saint John.

One night a neighbour came up to play cards with my brother and me and while we were playing I heard the same Sw-i-i-sh-sh sound I had heard as a child. It was coming from outside.

I didn't think anything of it at the time, I only remembered it later.

After the neighbour left, around ten o'clock, to walk the two miles to his home I heard a noise outside but my brother didn't see anything and a short time later I went to bed.

I remember hearing a strange scratching sound and sitting up in bed trying to scream but nothing happened, no sound came out. Then my bedroom lit up with a bright light that seemed to come from the outside.

The next thing I remember it was early the next morning and three brown forms were carrying me, more like floating me on air, back to my room. I remember the tallest one looked ugly and they didn't have hands, more like hoofs at the end of their arms.

Under hypnosis Hazel was able to remember a few more details of this experience. She remembers that after the bright light she was taken somewhere and she remembers looking up at the three figures who were lean-ing over her.

She was unable to define any features, save to re-iterate that the tallest of the three was "ugly" but she was surprised to discover that the brown of the figures was not skin but a seamless form-molding fabric.

I visited the site of her brother's former home near Barnesville. All that remains is the foundation in the still isolated location. We stopped at the site of the visit-ing neighbour's home and Hazel said she and her brother had talked to the neighbour's family who confirmed his arrival home at a time consistent with when he left that night.

"We thought it may have been him holding a big flashlight or something but he didn't even own a big light."

There were no other houses in the area then, in the mid-1940s, nor are there any more there now, in the mid-1990s.

There is literally a common ground between Ha-zel's experiences both in the 1930s and the 1940s and those of Bill Titus in the 1980s and his memory of his mother's mysterious sightings of an earlier time. Both Barnesville and Titusville are on the Hammond River and within a 10-mile radius of a still sparsely populated densely wooded area of Kings/St. John Counties.

When I met Hazel she told me she had heard from a relative that Bill Titus, too, "had seen something," but she did not know him, only knew of him.**dd**

What Bill Titus saw 20 years ago is still an Unidentified Flying Object

Amateur historian Bill Titus has lived most of his seventy-plus years among the rolling hills and valleys that straddle the Hammond River. Like all of Kings County the countryside around the small community of Titusville is lush and green and the residents, a blend of originals and newcomers, are bound by invisible ties of independence and generosity.

Bill still lives in the farmhouse where he was born. His life and notebooks are crammed with the things he has seen, heard and wondered about, among them strange sightings witnessed by him, friends and family. He is a man who still finds life filled with more questions than answers.

Take, for example, the evening of Saturday, May 14, 1977, *For the first time in my life I saw something I cannot explain,* he wrote in his notebook at the time.

I had come right home around eight o'clock from a grave (he had been digging) at Lakeside. Went out to feed cattle on the meadow, left tractor and trailer on meadow while I looked for a missing cow ... found her dead incidentally – she had a prolapsed uterus ... but mysteriously the calf had managed to survive. It must have suckled off her at some point because it was healthy."

Ralph Floyd, his friend and next door neighbour, walked down to where the tractor was and Bill met him there.

We looked at the new calf then I got on the tractor and Ralph sat on the side of the trailer, facing East as we came up the meadow. We were coming up fairly near and parallel to a bank when I saw to the East and a few degrees south, a strange light. It was in the tops of the trees ... I mean it appeared in the tops of the trees, about halfway to the Barnesville Road.

I first saw it through a screen of trees on the brook bank, the grove across the brook, but by backing up a few feet I could see it with only the far trees in the way. By this time it had sunk deeper into the screen of trees.

It sank from view in approximately 30 seconds, I did have time to shift gears and back up so maybe it was more like 60 seconds. Afterward I placed its location at approximately at a hardwood top visible in the dusk on the horizon.

What did it look like?

My first thought was the headlight of a plane, my second, the moon viewed through the trees. Because of the trees it was of indefinite shape.

I said to Ralph, "How high was it when you first saw it?

He said, 'In the tops of the trees.'

It was bright and an orangy yellow, more orange than the moon or a plane headlight, and it seemed to hover then slowly sink from view.

Ralph and I took the tractor and crossed the brook and left the tractor and trailer on the upper flat and walked in the woods road. Just before we got to the old pole track the darned thing appeared again about 100 yards southeast of us. This placed it on top of the steep bank at about tree top level. It seemed about the size of a baseball: round, brilliant orange-yellow, above it appeared a grey-white wispy substance.

My first thought was some sort of parachute har-
ness that had caught in a tree top. I think it more likely to
have been a wisp of smoke showing in the lights, it seemed
to have neither substance nor form.

The object, or light again seemed to remain sus-
pended for a time then slowly sank from view. I caught
one last glimpse of it through the evergreens that grow on
the slope at what must have been nearly ground level.

Only minutes later I got to the clearing at the top of
the hill after a mad scramble. There was nothing to be
seen. It was quite dark. The dog, who had come with me,
gave no evidence of sensing anything. On the heavy, damp
air – it had rained most of the day – I could smell Ralph's
cigarette and the match that he used but nothing else.

Was what we saw flares? Did they rise from the
ground? Did they come down from the sky?

I did not call out but Ralph and I talked freely and
our voices would have been heard for some distance. I
think a flare pistol makes a report and a flare from one
rises and falls. This thing appeared bright and motionless at tree top level, then slowly sank. There was no noise,
no smell. It did not appear to either rise or descend. It just
appeared and hung motionless then slowly sank from
sight still glowing.

The second flare for want of a better word, appeared
at about the location I had in mind as the sight of the first
flare. The thing was bright, gave the   impression of burning but not burning out. It was about the colour of a yellow bug bulb.

I am writing this while it is still fresh in my memory
– even now it seems, or begins to seem, like a dream – but
Ralph and I both saw it twice and I went puffing and
panting and scrambling through the brambles where a
rabbit wouldn't go in the dusk that became almost full
dark ere we got home!

Signed at 12:30 a.m. May 15, 1977 by J.W. Titus
        He added a p.s. to his notes:
        Mother, some years ago, saw a light of some kind in this same general area.

✳✳✳

Bill Titus has many interesting stories to tell of his observances over the years, living as he does in the comparative isolation of Titusville in Kings County. One of the most interesting of the phenomena he has observed, and one for which he has never found a reasonable explanation, occurred in the Fall of 1980 when he stepped out in his back yard one morning to be met by a blanket of some unknown substance covering a section of his property.

"It was as if during the night someone had sewn something by hand that had sprouted and grown in a space about 40 or 50 feet long, three or four feet wide and two feet thick. The edges sort of petered out, rather than being squared off.

"The material was of little globules, like very small pinkish peas with a tough skin and a thick, translucent jelly inside.

"I put one in my mouth but it had no taste.

"The phenomenon lasted for several days before it disappeared. Earl Jeffries and another fellow came by and I showed it to them but they couldn't figure out what it could be either. We looked around to see if there were any tracks that might be a clue to how it got there, maybe by a truck with a spreader on it ... but there was nothing."

Then around 10:50 p.m on May 29, 1982 he again saw something strange in the sky. A cigarette shaped cylinder high in the sky that looked to be the length of the space between the last two stars in the Big Dipper. The object gave the impression of moving away from his vision, rather than falling toward earth. He later learned that in all probability he had witnessed the disintegration of a Soviet Satellite.

Another time Bill watched fascinated as a little whirlwind picked up something that shone in the light like pieces of tinfoil then disappeared. dd

Sunset in West Saint John

Perc Elkin was curled up comfortably on a sofa in the living room of her home in the western outskirts of Saint John. Her husband, Ike, was mowing the lawn and son Peter was upstairs, studying for his final high school examinations.

Although she was reading the paper Perc was, as always, very aware of the sunset that filled the window every evening at dusk. The following is her story of a particular evening in June, she believes it was either in the year 1970 or 1971.dd

Perc Elkin's Story

The sun had set but the sky still glowed in the west when suddenly I became aware of this red light that came into the horizon. I thought to myself, 'there's the first star of the evening.'

But it was too big, too red. It had to be something else, maybe a plane ... except it wasn't moving although it was getting larger. I couldn't figure out what it could be and I called Peter to come downstairs and look. He couldn't figure it out either, so he went and got his telescope and set it up out on the deck.

Just as he focused on the object it split in two identi-

cal pieces, one piece streaked just like a shooting star down the Bay of Fundy coast but the rest of it came toward us.

We watched, fascinated as it came closer and closer, just above the tree tops, at a speed you would expect a plane to be travelling and it was the size of a small plane, but there was no noise. It was so close yet it was silent. Whatever it was, was solid grey and shaped like a boomerang, with no lights or anything that looked like a window, just flat, two dimensional grey.

Peter and I watched it go over the roof of the house and disappear behind the trees. I called Ike to come in and we told him all about it and he said maybe we should call and tell someone about it.

We decided to call the radio station, CFBC I think it was. We thought maybe someone else had seen it and they might have had some reports but they hadn't. They didn't seem very interested in what we had to offer.

It's really strange, you know. I told a lot of people about it and I asked a lot of people if they had seen anything that night but no one had. Peter and I were the only ones to see it, I guess.

Fredericton area sighting reported as book readied for printer

It was around 11:30 p.m. on March 3, 1996 that Elizabeth Peterson and her father saw strange lights in the sky near their Mazerolle Settlement home in the Fredericton area. Granted, they were tired. They were just arriving home from a trip to Ontario and it was late at night but the lights did seem strange ...

... but that wasn't the strangest aspect of this UFO sighting.

The strangest part was that neither Ms. Peterson or her father even remembered seeing the lights until 24 hours later!

"I find it strange that a memory lapse would happen to both of us," she told a reporter from the *Fredericton Gleaner.*

She said she was certain it was not a helicopter or aeroplane and it wasn't snowing, in fact the sky was quite clear at the time.

What they saw were steady lights in the sky that appeared to be moving along with the vehicle, hovering just above tree level.

"Dad thought it was strange before I did," she told the reporter. "The way the lights were situated it looked like they were square or oblong with two on the top and two on the bottom. I said maybe it's a weather balloon or something.

"The lights didn't look that bright from where I was sitting. After about a couple of minutes they disappeared. It sort of went over the top of us and was gone."

The newspaper story confirmed that officials at CFB Gagetown said there were no military helicopters or weather balloons in the sky that particular day and at that particular time.

Environment Canada official Dave Wartman also said to his knowledge there were no balloons from the weather service flying that evening although, conceivably, a weather balloon could come from anywhere. But he said it was unlikely they would have lights on them and more unlikely they would be flying at tree level.

There were no scheduled flights due at Fredericton Airport at that time.

The Peterson's was the only sighting reported on that night, a not unusual occurrence according to Stanton Friedman. He said often people will see something but not report it because they think they are the only ones who saw it.

Mr. Friedman told the reporter that ten per cent of those who attend his UFO lectures admit to having seen "a flying saucer" of some kind. dd

About the Author

Dorothy Dearborn began writing as a child and published her first poetry and short stories in the 1950s. A television career in the 1960s, was interrupted by six years of active politics.

She worked as a reporter and later served as city editor of *The Evening Times-Globe* and was editor of the weekly newspapers *The Kings County Record* and *The Saint John Citizen.*

Among her many interests are the promotion of literacy in New Brunswick and acting as chair of the Southern New Brunswick Area Legal Aid Appeal Board and a frustrating romance with Duplicate Bridge.

Mrs. Dearborn continues to work as a journalist. Her articles are regularly published in newspapers and magazines nationally and internationally.

When not searching out stories for her articles and books she can be found in front of her Macintosh computer at the family's 19th Century farm house in Hampton, in the company of her aging Newfoundland Dog, *Tillie*, an equally ancient pony named *Soupy* and a motly assortment of other critters, among them a rooster named *Rocky.*

She is married to Fred Dearborn, they have four grown children and several grandchildren.

About the Illustrator

Carol Taylor of Rothesay is a New Brunswick figurative artist who works primarily in clay and oil. Her figurehead clock design graces the Germain Street entrance to the Saint John City Market. *Ageratas Complete*, a major work, has met with wide critical acclaim throughout New Brunswick.